LOOKING AFTER YOUR CAT

HAMLYN HELP YOURSELF GUIDE

LOOKING AFTER YOUR CAT

WENDY GOSS

HAMLYN

First published in 1990 by
The Hamlyn Publishing Group Limited,
a division of the Octopus Publishing Group,
Michelin House, 81 Fulham Road,
London SW3 6RB

Some material in this book first appeared in
The Complete Book of the Cat, 1984
Copyright © Octopus Books Limited, 1984

ISBN 0 600 56878 4

Printed and bound in Great Britain
by Collins, Glasgow

Contents

Introduction

Centuries of domestication have never managed to rob the cat of its independence. It will accept food and shelter from its human owners and consent to abide by the house rules, so long as they do not go against its basic nature, but it is never subservient and it will never become a piece of property. Unlike a dog, it will not remain loyal to unkind or neglectful owners; it is quite capable of walking out on you and finding itself another home. If it becomes a stray, it will soon polish up its predatory skills and fend for itself. Though your cat may seem like a cuddly bundle of fur most of the time, if its territory is challenged or it needs to defend itself, it can turn into a snarling, spitting fury, the legacy of its wild ancestors plain to see.

So long as you give a cat the sort of home it requires, it will give you years of pleasure in return. Whether it is an aristocratic Siamese or a rugged moggie, a cat is the most beautiful of pets. Its design could hardly be bettered: it is a stealthy and swift hunter and an efficient catcher of vermin, as well as a clean and fastidious house guest and a relaxing companion for a stressed owner, whose blood pressure and pulse rate decrease as a rhythmic stroking produces a throaty, soothing purr.

Choosing the right type of cat for your lifestyle, providing the correct diet and care from the very beginning, understanding its needs and instincts, and learning to spot the early signs of illness so that you can take the necessary action, will all help you to keep your pet fit and happy and enjoy a close and rewarding relationship for the whole of your cat's lifetime.

1

Choosing your Cat

You may never have to choose your cat – it may choose you. Many fond owners can tell you about the day when a cat's bright eyes and eager whiskers appeared round the door, examined and approved their home, then settled in. Such lodgers often defy all attempts to dislodge them and the most vigorous efforts to restore them to their original owners may be in vain. For most of us, however, choosing a cat means taking a number of decisions: male or female, kitten or fully-grown cat, long or short-haired, pedigree or non-pedigree and whether or not you plan to breed or show. As your pet will be part of the family for many years, it makes sense to think hard and well.

Cat or kitten

Few creatures are as winsome as a pretty, playful kitten but kittens need a great deal of time and attention so in a busy household, a home where everyone is out at work all day or where the owners are elderly, it may be more sensible to acquire a fully grown cat. If you take an adult cat from an owner who can no longer care for it, you have the advantage of knowing something of its history and temperament; if you take a cat from a sanctuary, you are giving a loving home to a needy animal and may well be saving its life. An older cat will be more independent and more staid than a kitten and though it may take longer to settle in, love and patience will normally win the day. The main disadvantage with an adult cat is that its habits will already be formed. If you find yourself with a cat that has been accustomed to roaming in search of adventure, you cannot expect it to change its nature and sit quietly by the fire, simply because you have given it a home. A cat that has been badly treated in the past will not trust you immediately; it will have to learn slowly that life has taken an upturn.

One cat or two

You may also want to think carefully about taking two cats at the same time. Two companion cats eat better and are more relaxed than a single cat; they will keep one another company when you are out or on holiday, play with one another when you are too busy to take notice of them and remain firm friends for the whole of their lives. If they arrive together, or within a short time of one another, you will avoid all problems of jealousy, when one cat feels that its territory has been invaded by a newcomer. They will chase one another, tumble and wrestle and fall asleep with their arms around one another. Two litter mates are ideal; they can comfort and reassure one another in their new surroundings. If two kittens come from different litters they may make a great show of hissing and spitting but they will usually make friends quite quickly. As an owner, you will find that you get a great deal of extra pleasure and amusement from the antics of two cats, as they will probably have quite different personalities and temperaments.

To breed or not to breed

Unless you plan to breed, it is wise to have you pet neutered. A full tom is not a suitable household pet; he will mark his territory thoroughly, which means that your house will smell strongly of urine; he will roam the local rooftops at night getting into fights and making you unpopular with the neighbours and he will probably disappear for days at a time. An unneutered queen can be a full-time job when she is on heat; she will make a great deal of fuss and noise and will battle to escape and find a mate at every opportunity. You will either have to batten down the hatches, fasten every door and window and watch her desperate frustration or allow her to have litter after litter of mongrel kittens.

If you plan to have your pet neutered, it matters little which sex you choose, though many owners claim that neutered males are steadier and more placid than neutered females, though you do need to watch their diet as some tend to put on weight.

When you have breeding in mind, you will need to buy the best female you can afford of the chosen breed. If possible, buy two females of the same age and preferably from the same background, but from different bloodlines. These will form a good foundation for your own strain in generations to come. Never buy a 'breeding pair' of cats. Of course, you cannot breed kittens without using both a male and a female but you can take your female to a carefully selected stud male at the appropriate time and if the resulting litter is not top quality, you can use a different male for the next litter. Keeping a stud male is a job for the very experienced breeder, not the novice, so do not be tempted beyond your capabilities.

Pedigree or non-pedigree

Pedigree cats are comparatively new, as it was only in 1871 that records were first kept and pedigrees produced. 'Moggies', or mongrels, come in all sorts of colour combinations and they are usually healthy and sturdy, self-reliant and earlier to mature than many pedigrees. They are just as affectionate, lively and cuddly as cats with impressive ancestry, and the years of pleasure they will give do not depend on a pedigree certificate.

Of course, choosing a specific breed does mean that you know what your kitten will look like as an adult and roughly what size it will be. You can also choose a breed that is likely to have the type of temperament you prefer – but remember that every cat is an individual and it can turn out very different from what you expect: a highly strung Persian, for instance, or a docile and placid Siamese.

You can see most of the available breeds by visiting cat shows. Most major towns have several shows a year and you can find them through adverts in the cat press or on local radio. At the show you can wander around the pens until you see a breed that appeals to you, then talk to one of the owners. You will usually find them only too willing to talk at length about their favourite subject but remember that they are biased and likely to think their cat's breed the best of all, so you will need to ask the right questions to find the right type of cat for you.

Coat length will be largely a matter of preference but remember that long-haired cats need grooming once or twice every single day, otherwise their coats will becomes matted. Because they are kept in warm homes they moult all through the year, so if you cannot find the necessary grooming and cleaning time, a short-haired cat will prove a better choice.

Pedigree Longhairs

These are splendid looking cats, elegant and decorative and very hardy, in spite of their exotic appearance. They require more attention than the Shorthairs and if you plan to show them, they do need protection from too much sun or damp, as both can have a bad effect on their coats.

Persians
Persians are gentle, intelligent cats with a quiet disposition. They love to be fussed over and adjust quite easily to an indoor life. Their fur is long and silky and they have cobby bodies on short, sturdy legs and short, fluffy tails. Their heads are broad and round, noses short and broad, ears small and well-shaped and eyes big and round.
Black. One of the oldest pedigree Longhairs, the Black Persian is difficult to breed to show standard, especially as the fur tends to fade or turn rusty looking if the cat spends too much time in the sun. It should have jet black fur and copper coloured eyes. It can be hard to judge colour in kittens; those with a rusty colour may develop jet black coats within six months or so.
Blue Persian. The most popular of the Longhairs has very long fur and deep orange eyes. Colours vary: most are greyish blue, some are nearer true grey, others are lavender or deep sapphire.

Once again, it is difficult to judge colour in kittens. Those who seem to have the best colour may change as they grow and those with tabby markings may lose them as they shed their baby coat and turn out to have a splendid colour. Too much sunlight can give the coat a brownish hue.

Cream and Blue-Cream. Creams have silky coats, any colour from pale to medium cream and should be as uniform a colour as possible. Sometimes their coats can be too reddish. Blue-Creams are almost always females, with the occasional male likely to be sterile. The British standard is a soft blue and cream which intermingle softly but the American standard requires distinct cream and blue patches.

White. A very popular type with soft and silky coats. The eye colours vary and may be orange or blue. Blue eyes can be a warning of deafness, so owners need to watch for signs. There is a type with one blue and one orange eye and in this case, the blue does not seem to denote deafness.

Red. A rare type because it is very difficult to breed a good colour without tabby markings but good specimens have rich red coats and large copper eyes.

Tabby. It has been hard to breed Longhairs with clear markings but apart from the rich, tawny sable of the Brown Tabby, there is a Silver type, which has pale silver fur with black markings and a Red, with rich red fur and deeper red markings.

Tortoiseshell. These are rare because they are almost all female, with the occasional male being sterile, so they are difficult to breed. They are beautiful cats with patched black, red and cream fur. The Tortoiseshell and White has similar coloured fur but with white patches on the lower part of the body.

Smoke. These can be Black or Blue shading to silver at the roots, with a silver ruff and ear tufts. Kittens are born Black or Blue and the shading begins to appear from about three weeks.

Bi-Colour or Cameo. Their long coats have two colours, with an off-white to cream base tipped with another colour.

Chinchillas or Silver Persian. These extremely beautiful cats have great self-confidence and very sweet natures. In spite of their dainty and delicate looks they are very hardy. At first glance, they appear to be self-coloured but a closer look shows that their silver-white fur is tipped with black on the back, flanks, ears and tail.

Colourpoint. These are known as Himalayans in the USA and they have the build and coat of the Persian with the colouring and marking of a Siamese. They have pale body fur, with the dark face, ears, legs and tail and the blue eyes of the Siamese, though these are round, not oriental. Quite a range of colours is available: Blue, Chocolate, Lilac, Red and Tortoiseshell.

Turkish cats

These cats were first introduced from Turkey in the 1960s. They are affectionate, intelligent and willing to go anywhere with their owners. The most unusual thing about them is their liking for swimming and they will even enjoy a pleasantly warm bath. They are not known as good mousers.

Turkish cats have long silky coats in winter but lose a good deal of fur in summer, so that they can look almost short-haired. They are white with auburn markings on the face and tail and amber eyes. Their bodies are medium-sized, long and sturdy, their ears are large and upright and their eyes round and quite widely spaced.

Birman

The Birman, or Sacred Cat of Burma, is a very old breed, said to have been the guardian of Burmese temples in ancient times and believed to possess the souls of dead priests. They are gentle cats who like people and other animals.

Their colouring is similar to Colourpoints but they have distinctive white feet like gloves: front paws have white gloves ending in a line across at the third joint, hind paws have white gloves covering the entire paw and ending in a point that extends up the back of the hocks. Other types available are Blue Point, Chocolate Point, Lilac Point, Red Point and Tortie Point. There should always be a good contrast between body and points colour.

Their heads are broad and round, they have sloping foreheads and Roman noses and their ears are a little larger than most Longhairs. Coats are silky, with a heavy neck ruff and a tendency to curl on the stomach. The fur does not mat.

Maine Coon

Bred in the USA for over a century, and natives of the state of Maine, these cats were called 'Coon' because their fur resembled that of a raccoon. Their fur is heavy and shaggy, shorter on the shoulders and longer on the stomach and hindlegs, so that it looks as though they wear breeches. Tabby is the most usual colour but there are many others and the eyes may be any shade of green, gold or copper. They are placid but rather shy and make good mousers but they do not adapt well to an indoor life and need space to roam.

They are medium to large cats, strong and broad-chested, with large round paws. The eyes are large and wide apart and the long, tapering tail has flowing hair.

Shorthaired cats

The Shorthairs need far less attention than Longhairs and though they are less spectacular cats, they have their own unique character. They make undemanding and delightful family pets.

British Shorthairs

These are the pedigree descendants of the cats that arrived in Britain in Roman times and are bred in similar colours to the Longhairs. They are powerful, sturdily-built cats, with well-knit bodies of medium length and broad chests. Heads are broad and round with full cheeks, small ears spaced well apart, short straight noses and large round eyes. The short, dense coats should have no harshness about them.

They are good-natured, intelligent and affectionate cats with a truly British character – they need time to get to know strangers before they offer friendship. They have a mind of their own but are fairly adaptable.

Blue. The most popular of the British Shorthairs is a very handsome cat with bluish grey fur, which should be as even in colour as possible, with no white or tabby markings anywhere. The colour sets off the rich copper or orange eyes.

Tabby. Most follow the basic marbled pattern, with three dark stripes running down the spine, an M shaped dark marking on the head and a pair of unbroken lines down the chest, known as 'mayoral chains'. Rings or bands should be clearly marked on the tail and legs and a good specimen will have clearly marked spectacles round the eyes. Another form of Tabby has mackerel marking, sometimes known as the tiger pattern, with a central line running down the spine and numerous narrow lines running from spine to middle. Tabbies may come in the classic Brown, or Silver or Red (when the background colour should be rich red rather than ginger).

Spotted. These striking cats have a coat pattern rather like that of the Mackerel Tabby, but broken up into spots. The spots must be distinct but may be round, rosette shaped or oblong. The most popular types are Silver with black spots, Brown with black spots or Red with deep red spots.

Tortoiseshell. This is a popular type, almost exclusively female. The black, dark and light red patches should be clear and distinct, without white hairs or tabby markings and the legs, tail, ears and feet should be well patched. There are problems with choosing a kitten because the patches often do not appear clearly until the cat matures. Cats that turn out to be well-marked may be quite dark as kittens.

Tortoiseshell and White. This is an all-female variety and it is hard to breed to get a good colour standard. The patches should be clear and well-defined and the colours brilliant and they should cover the head, ears and cheeks as well as the tail, back and part of the flanks. White should never predominate.

Bi-Coloured. There are various colours – black and white, orange and white, blue and white, cream and white – and up to two-thirds of the coat should be coloured, with patches of colour clear and evenly distributed. The face should be patched and a white blaze is desirable.

White. These are supposed to be pure white, untinged with yellow and there are three different eye colours: blue or orange or odd-eyed, with one eye of each colour. All the kittens are born with blue eyes. Odd-eyed cats have no hearing problems but those with blue eyes do need careful watching.

Cream. It is hard to breed a Cream Shorthair with no trace of white and no markings of any kind. Kittens sometimes lose white as they mature.

Black. Coats should be jet black to the roots with no rusty tinge and they suffer from the same problems as Longhairs if they are exposed to too much sun. Kittens may lose tabby markings or brownish hue as they mature.

Manx

Said to have descended from cats that swam ashore to the Isle of Man from the wrecked galleons of the Spanish Armada, the Manx cat is never likely to be mistaken for another breed. The perfect Manx has no tail at all but a slight hollow at the end of the backbone, and is called a Rumpy; those with a short stump of a tail are called Stumpy. Some Manx cats do have offspring with tails. They make very good pets, very affectionate, adaptable and confident, easily trained and willing to walk on a lead. Their soft voices are more like a squeak.

They have short, solid, compact bodies with broad chests and long back legs, so that the rump is higher than the shoulders. This gives them a bobbing gait and the nickname of the 'rabbit cat'. The short dense coat gives the Manx the feeling of being padded and there is a wide variety of colours and markings.

Rex

Sometimes called poodle cats, the distinctive Rex has a short, plush coat that waves and curls, and even the whiskers and eyebrows are crinkled. The Cornish Rex appeared in 1950 and the Devon Rex in 1960. The change in coats from that of other cats was caused by mutations – a sudden variation that appears in an animal for no apparent reason. A careful breeding programme showed that it was possible to produce kittens with similar coats but the two varieties did not mix.

They may be any colour and they are very easy to groom. Hard hand grooming will keep them looking good, with an occasional combing with a small-toothed metal comb to remove dust or fleas.

The Rex cats are very energetic, playful and mischievous;

they are great characters and do not like to be ignored.

Cornish. Their short, plush coats curl, wave and ripple over the whole of the body. They have small, rather narrow heads with oval eyes spaced wide apart, and hard muscular bodies standing high on long, slender legs.

Devon. Their heads are wedge-shaped with full cheeks, a pixie-like expression and huge bat ears, and noses with a definite stop or bend in the middle. Short, fine fur, soft and wavy, covers their slender, muscular bodies so the Devon Rex can look very bare after a moulting period.

Siamese

These true aristocrats of the cat world came to Britain in 1884 from the Royal Palace in Bangkok, as a gift to the British consul general. Originally they were frail and difficult to rear but eventually they became acclimatized. They are very sociable cats, needing a great deal of love and attention and though they normally enjoy the company of other pets, they can be demanding and jealous of rivals. They often turn into one-person cats and there is no predicting which member of the family they will select.

They have an exotic appearance with light coloured bodies and dark points – face, ears, legs and tails. Their heads are long and well-proportioned with ears large and pricked, bodies long and svelte on slim legs, tails long and tapering. They have deep blue, almond-shaped eyes. All Siamese kittens are born white and only begin to show markings and colourings after a week or so.

Seal Point. These are the original Siamese cats, with cream bodies and seal brown points.

Blue Point. This was the second variety recognized, and registered in about 1890. The coat is snowy white, shading to light blue on the back. The points are bluish – though this is often more of a slate grey.

Chocolate Point. This was only recognized as a distinct breed in the 1950s. It is a difficult colour to breed and the final colouring is only reached when the kitten is past a year old. Temperature changes and too much sun can affect the colouring, which should be ivory, with milk chocolate points.

Lilac Point. The coat is off-white or magnolia (milk white in the USA) with pinkish grey points.

Red Point. Introduced by a cross between a Siamese and a Red Tabby Shorthair, it took years to breed out traces of Tabby while keeping the character of the Siamese. A good specimen has a white coat with any shading to apricot towards the back. The face, ears and tail are reddish-gold with the legs and feet nearer to apricot.

Tortie Point. These are the result of a cross between a Seal Point and a Red Point and are nearly always female. The points may be speckled black, red and cream, with the basic colours of Seal, Blue, Chocolate and Lilac.

Tabby Point. This has only recently been recognised as a breed. The body should be pale and unmarked – Cream, Lilac, Blue, Chocolate and Red – and the points have typical tabby markings.

Cream Point. The body colour is warm white and the face and legs are the colour of clotted cream, while the ears, nose and tail are nearer to apricot.

Havana Brown

This graceful creature has never been crossed with other breeds and has established its own niche in the cat world. It is mahogany brown, with a glossy, fine coat that needs the minimum of grooming to keep it looking beautiful. Its body is long and lithe, on slim dainty legs. The head is long, the ears large, and the oriental shaped eyes start blue and turn green after six months.

Havanas are extroverts, affectionate and entertaining, less vocal than Siamese and with quieter voices. They need to be protected from cold and damp.

Egyptian Mau

Probably descended directly from the cats of ancient Egypt, the Egyptian Mau is said to be the only natural breed of domesticated spotted cat. It makes a robust and playful pet, with a dog-like devotion to its owners.

Markings are quite distinctive, with random spots on the body, a dorsal stripe over the haunches running to the tip of the tail and 'vest button' spots on the underbody. Coats are silky and fine but dense to the touch and there are three colours – Silver, with charcoal markings; Bronze, with dark brown markings; and Smoke, with black markings. Conformation is midway between the Siamese and the Shorthair with muscular medium-length bodies, and hindlegs longer than forelegs. The large, almond-shaped eyes are gooseberry green.

Abyssinians

These intelligent, friendly and playful cats make very good pets; they are quiet, they travel well in cars and like to go anywhere with their owners but they do not take well to confinement and will not enjoy being shut indoors while their owners are out at work.

The coat, with its short, fine fur, is their most distinguishing feature. The standard Abyssinian is known as the Ruddy Abyssinian but the name does not do justice to the subtle colouring: a ruddy brown coat is ticked with dark black or brown bands. The Reds are lustrous copper-red with no black in their coats, ticked with brown or dark red, and the Blues are a soft, warm blue-grey ticked with deeper steel blue. Most have a lighter colour around the lips and lower jaws, but if it extends down the neck it is a fault.

They have firm, lithe, muscular bodies with broad heads tapering to a fine wedge. Their ears are comparatively large and tufted and their eyes, large and expressive, are amber, hazel or green.

Russian Blue

The 'Ruskies' may or may not have come originally from Russia, though it is said that they first arrived in Britain as a gift from a Russian Tzar. Whatever their origin, careful breeding has produced the graceful cats seen at shows today. Their fur is short and dense, clear blue with a silvery sheen. Their bodies are long and lithe with slender legs, dainty oval feet and long, tapering tails. The short head is wedge-shaped, with long pointed ears and vivid green eyes.

They make fine pets, being quiet-voiced and undemanding, loyal and loving. They can live happily in a flat and are very hardy.

Burmese

Early breeding took place in America, where the breed was recognized in the mid-30s, then after World War II it arrived in Britain and steadily grew in popularity. They are intelligent, extrovert cats with distinct personalities and can easily rule the household if they are not well-trained as kittens. They are very playful and good with children but they are better kept in pairs.

The American Burmese have rounder heads and cobbier bodies than those bred in Britain, where faces should be wedge-shaped with large, lustrous eyes set wide apart, which can be any shade of yellow from chartreuse to amber. Legs are slender but in proportion to the body, with the back legs a little longer than the front and straight, medium-length tails. The coat is short and satiny and though in the USA only the Brown is considered true Burmese, there are several other colours.

Brown. This should be warm sable or rich seal-brown all over, gradually shading to a paler colour on the chest and belly and a little darker on the ear tips.

Chocolate. This is a fairly recent colour variation. The basic colour is warm milk chocolate, the more even the better, though the face and ears tend to be darker.

Blue. Another less common colour, where the coat is soft silver grey, slightly darker on the back and tail. The glossy coat gives the colour a silvery sheen on ears, face and feet.

Lilac. Pale dove grey with a slightly pinkish coat and often slightly darker face and ears. The nose and paw pads are lavender pink.

Red. This came from breeding between a Red Tabby and a Red Point Siamese. The coat is pale tangerine with darker ears and there may be slight tabby markings on the face and elsewhere.

Tortoiseshell. These are almost always female. The coat may be a mix of brown and red, blue and cream, chocolate and light red, lilac and cream.

Cream. A rich cream colour with slighty darker ears and paws with small marks on the face and elsewhere and pink nose and paw pads.

Korat

Known in north-eastern Thailand for centuries, where it was always much prized, the Korat has only been available outside that country in recent years and the numbers in Britain are comparatively small. They are happy, friendly and gentle cats with sweet natures and quiet voices. They are usually devoted to their owners and make good companions. They are not prolific breeders, so you may have to wait for a kitten.

Their heart-shaped faces are unusual, the heads small with large ears, bodies medium length. The fur is silver-blue, tipped with silver and the large, luminous eyes are brilliant green.

Where to buy

You may find pedigree kittens for sale at a cat show, but resist the temptation to buy there and then. The stress of the long day out, following so soon after an intensive weaning and vaccination programme may mean that the kittens are off-colour for a few days. If they go back home to their usual environment, this soon wears off but if you bear them off to a new home, however loving, they may be overwhelmed and their development may be affected. If you fall for a particular kitten at a show, then pay a deposit and arrange to collect it ten days later, when it has recovered from its outing and you have had a chance to get everything ready.

Buy pedigree kittens from a reputable breeder, preferably one who brings up the kittens in the house so that they get used to the noises of normal family life, rather than in outside pens. Cat show catalogues usually have advertisements from breeders, or you can find out the address of the breed society and contact them for a list. Other possibilities are advertisements in the magazine *Cat World* or in newspapers. For popular breeds, you may have to put your name on a waiting list and any good breeder will want to know something about your household and your outlook, so that they can be sure they are sending their kittens to good, caring homes. It is a good idea to visit the breeder even before the kittens arrive, to make sure that the cats are healthy and happy and to get some idea of the temperament of the mother-to-be.

Be very careful about buying from a pet shop. Kittens do far better if they go straight from their mother to a new home, rather than spending days being stared at and handled by endless strangers, and infection can spread very quickly in a shop. If you do buy from a shop, make sure that it is spotlessly clean and that the animals are really healthy and lively. Check if you have the option of returning the kitten in a few days if any health problems develop – though you may not be able to bear parting from your kitten anyway, it shows that the shop is confident about the quality of the animals they sell. Sometimes shops act as agents for breeders and may be able to put you in touch with someone who has kittens for sale.

Non-pedigree kittens can be obtained sometimes from animal sanctuaries and sanctuaries always have more adult cats than available homes. The cats will normally be examined by a veterinary surgeon to make sure that they are in good health and the sanctuary will often make a small charge or ask for a donation, to help them carry on their work. Sometimes they will ask to inspect your home and you should not resent this; it shows how keen they are to do the best for the animals.

If you have any difficulty in finding a non-pedigree kitten, you might try asking the local vet, who will sometimes know of litters needing homes. Otherwise, put a 'wanted' advertisement in the local paper and you may find that your phone is ringing all evening.

What to look for

The same basic rules apply, whether you are choosing a pedigree or non-pedigree cat. You will want a healthy kitten, fully ready to leave its mother. It is essential that it is fully weaned, which means that it has been on solid food for several weeks and totally removed from its mother's milk for at least a fortnight. If a kitten is still drinking a good deal of mother's milk, then is suddenly removed to a new environment, it can easily develop gastritis. Never take a kitten before 7 weeks: mongrel cats often leave their mothers at 8 or 9 weeks while 10 to 12 weeks is normal for pedigrees.

If you are looking at pedigree kittens, ask the breeder about the good and bad points, so that you learn more about your chosen type of cat. If you are interested in breeding or showing, then make sure that the breeder knows this. Some breeders charge a set price for all their kittens, others charge more for possible show quality animals with 'pet quality' being cheaper. It is unwise to set out to look for a bargain. Most breeders are in the business for love rather than profit and bringing up a litter is an expensive business so that, on the whole, the prices charged are reasonable. On the other hand, it is only sensible to talk to more than one breeder, to get an idea of the 'going rate' for a particular breed.

Try to see the whole litter of kittens with the mother. If you have a choice of several kittens, it is sensible to choose the most lively and extrovert of the bunch, the one who comes gamboling out to meet you, inquisitive and playful. Quite often you will find that one of the kittens takes to you immediately and the choice is taken out of your hands. The small, shy kitten who always gets the worst of any confrontation with its littermates is not the right choice if you have a houseful of pets and children already but many owners who have gone against all the received wisdom and chosen the 'runt' of the litter have found that the extra time and patience it takes to make friends with a timid kitten is well worth while.

When you have found a kitten you like, check it over carefully to make sure it is healthy. Approach it gently, talking to it reassuringly, and you can make most of your inspection under the guise of stroking. Leave the mouth until last, as the kitten may want to struggle away after you have opened its mouth and peered inside. Before agreeing to buy, make sure your kitten comes up to the following standards:

Body. This should be firm, with the ribs and hips well-covered and no sign of a potbelly. Look under the tail for any yellowish staining, which could indicate that the kitten is suffering from diarrhoea.

Skin. A kitten's skin should be like a loose overcoat and if you lift the skin at the scruff of the neck very gently between your thumb and forefinger, it should spring back into place as soon as you let go. There should be no scabs or odd bumps.

Coat. Look carefully behind the ears and at the base of the spine for tell-tale gritty specks that could indicate flea infestation. The coat should feel soft to the touch and should smell fresh.

Eyes. These should be bright and clear with no sign of discharge and no third eyelid showing at the inner corner.

Ears. The inside should look clean and slightly moist. Dark grits may be caused by ear mites.

Mouth. The inside should be pink and clean with sharp white teeth. Look out for any signs of soreness or ulceration. Any offensive smell on the breath is a bad sign.

Nose. There should be no sign of discharge.

Behaviour. Healthy kittens are bright, playful and alert. If they are dull and listless and are obviously unhappy about being handled, they may be sickening for something.

If you are thinking of taking two kittens, sit and watch the littermates for a while and try to choose the two who tend to play most together.

2

The New Kitten

Arriving at its new home is an enormous adventure for a tiny kitten. It is in a strange place, with unfamiliar smells, without the reassurance of its mother or the rest of the litter. It is up to you, as the owner, to make the transition as smooth and stress-free as possible for your pet. Kittens are naturally sociable and inquisitive and, so long as you are prepared to take some time and trouble over the settling-in period, neither you nor your kitten should have any problems.

Preparing for your kitten

Having a kitten in the house is rather like having an inquisitive toddler, except that a kitten is far more agile. You will need to guard against much the same dangers, with perhaps a fire-guard in front of an open fire, the wires of electrical appliances either looped high or disconnected. Clear up tiny oddments like paper clips, safety pins, needles and above all tempting rubber bands. Toxic substances will need to be shut away where they cannot be knocked over and fish tanks covered. Kittens can squeeze into amazingly small spaces, so it is quite a good idea to block off spaces behind refrigerators, cookers and central heating boilers wherever possible, especially if the kitten is likely to have access to them when it is left alone. If you have a chest of drawers without a solid back, your kitten will soon find its way in and pack itself away in a drawer so either nail a piece of cardboard across the back or make certain that the drawers contain nothing harmful or likely to be suffocating.

You will need a certain amount of basic equipment for your kitten but it does not need to cost a great deal. The essentials are as follows:

Carrier. This may well be the most expensive item. You will need a carrier to collect your kitten as you should not think of allowing it loose in the car, where it may easily panic and fly onto your shoulder just as you are negotiating a difficult bend. Planning to carry it home inside your coat is a very bad idea – a bark from a passing dog and your kitten may streak off down the road, never to be seen again.

You can buy a cardboard carrier, which packs flat and is easily assembled quite cheaply from a pet shop but, though this will be perfectly adequate to collect your kitten, it will not last long. Even if you do not plan to travel frequently with your cat, you will need a carrier for trips to the vet, or to the cattery when you go on holiday, so it is probably a wise investment to begin by buying a sturdy carrier that will give years of service.

There are several types to choose from, in various shapes and designs. If you are sure that you will only be taking your cat on very short journeys, a vinyl 'holdall', designed with a clear window at one end and ventilation holes, might be sufficient but it is not suitable for long trips. The plastic-covered mesh carriers are easy to clean and have the advantage that the cat can see all round, so that it does not have to be suspicious about what is happening outside. However, you will need a cover over them if you are likely to be carrying them about in the cold or wet. Plastic and fibreglass carriers are warm and draught-proof as well as being easy to clean, though they may have condensation problems if you travel for long distances. A wicker basket is attractive and can double as a bed, but is much harder to clean and needs a wrapper round the outside to keep out draughts in cold weather.

On the whole, a top opening is preferable; it is much easier to get a reluctant cat in and out. Buy a carrier that will be large enough for the adult cat, or it will soon be redundant. Line it with several sheets of newspaper and then make a 'nest' of blanket or old sweaters, so that the kitten will feel secure.

Bed. You do not have to buy a bed for your kitten at this stage; in fact, it is wiser to find out what its sleeping habits are likely to be before spending the money. Some cats ignore the sumptuous sleeping arrangements provided by their owners and choose the floor, a hard chair or shelf instead. A cardboard box is ideal to begin with; start with a small box, so that the kitten feels enclosed and protected. Cut a door in the front so that the kitten can step in and out easily, then line it with newspaper, like the carrier, and make a cosy mattress out of soft material, pulled up round the sides of the box. This makes a draught-proof bed, disposable as soon as it gets soiled. Stand the box in a quiet corner, where the kitten can retire undisturbed if it is nervous or unsure.

Sanitary tray. Even if you will eventually expect your cat to perform outside, at least in the daytime, a tray is a necessity in the beginning. It should be shallow, so that the kitten can step into it easily and have enough litter to allow the kitten to dig. Stand the tray on newspaper in its permanent position, as moving it around will only confuse the kitten, which may use the spot where the tray used to be, confident that it is doing the right thing. If you have a very large home or your house is several storeys high, you may need more than one tray once your kitten has the run of the premises. If the tray is too far away, it may not always be able to find its way back in time.

There are several different styles, beginning with a basic open tray in various sizes (if you are taking two cats and expect them to share a tray, choose a large one). Another type has a ring of plastic that snaps around the bottom and helps to prevent litter being spread round the floor as the cat scratches vigorously, but a small kitten may find it hard to climb in. A third type has a hood enclosing the whole pan, with a hole at the front for entry. Some cats prefer the privacy afforded by these trays and they also help to contain the smell.

In the early days, you would be wise to use the same type of litter used by the breeder but later you can choose between proprietary cat litter, granules or wood-based variety (expensive but good for absorbing moisture and smells), or peat moss. If you choose to use inexpensive peat, you can put it in the middle of the compost heap whenever you clear the tray, so that the heat can kill the germs and after a few months, when it is well rotted, it can go on the garden.

Some owners change litter after every use but if you are not that rich, you will also need a scoop for removing the 'nasties'.

Food and water bowls. Dishes should be shallow and stand firmly on the floor. A kitten will find it harder to lap from a deep bowl and a saucer tips up too easily. Your cat should never use your plates or bowls; it should have its own dishes, which are washed (separately from those of the family) after every meal.

Toys. Play is very important for a kitten, improving its co-ordination and sharpening its reflexes. Pet shops have a range of cat toys but there are plenty of cheaper alternatives, many of them more satisfactory and safer than toys with tiny bells and lengths of elastic that might harm a kitten intent on chewing everything. Soft rubber and plastic should also be avoided. You will find that a piece of crumpled paper can give hours of fun, either bowled along the floor or swung back and forth on the end of a string. Few cats can resist a newspaper; it makes a good rustling noise and can be burrowed in and hurled around. If you are reading it at the time, that seems to add spice to the game. Never let kittens play with plastic bags; they may suffocate or chew off pieces and swallow them.

Table tennis balls bounce in unexpected directions and are easy for tiny paws to bat around and a 'spider' made from four pipe cleaners, laid across each other and securely bound round the middle, makes a popular plaything. Kittens love to play with something they can hold between their front legs, while they bring up their back legs to give it a thorough pounding and a mouse-shaped toy seems to be ideal – even the tiniest kitten seems to recognize it as a natural prey. You can buy clockwork mice but this is not a good idea for a new kitten – some youngsters find them quite frightening.

A couple of cardboard boxes from the supermarket can be fitted together and turned into an exciting play house for small kittens; simply fit two different sizes together, cut holes at various levels on each side and, if you wish, cover it with spongeable paper.

Scratching post. Cats need to exercise the muscles and tendons that control their claws and to remove the outer shell of worn claws. Out of doors, they will use tree trunks but inside they are likely to use your furniture, unless you provide them with a good alternative. You can buy a scratching post from the pet shop but many of them are too small to be useful once the cat is full grown and likes to stretch its full length as it claws. Larger and more effective scratching posts can be found through advertisements in the cat press or seen at shows, but they are quite expensive. The type that is angled at 65° seems very popular with cats.

If you prefer, you can make your own scratching post. A good sized log, anchored firmly, will make a good tree substitute but it may not add much to your room decor. Alternatively you can fix a good sized piece of wood to the wall in a quiet corner with a countersunk screw, then use heavy duty adhesive to fix hessian or carpet onto it. The covering can then be renewed whenever necessary.

Remember that one of the reasons that your cat always picks your favourite armchair to scratch is because it smells strongly of you. A well-worn sweater wrapped around the new scratching post for a couple of days before use can be a useful ploy.

Brush and comb. Shorthaired kittens will need grooming with a fine-toothed comb and perhaps a soft brush. Longhairs need a stiff brush and a wide-toothed metal comb. If you begin grooming your kitten right from the beginning – even if it is short-haired and needs the minimum of attention – it will be used to the process and grooming sessions will always be a pleasure for both owner and pet.

Collecting your kitten

Plan to collect your kitten at a quiet time, when there is as little as possible going on at home and when the children are out of the way, so that the kitten will have time to explore and get its bearings before having to cope with family life. Christmas and children's birthdays are bad times to introduce a kitten, as

28

everyone will be busy and over-excited and a tiny kitten may be upset and frightened.

Make sure that you know what diet your kitten has been given up to now, so that you can give the same food, at least at first. Any changes should be made gradually, to avoid gastric upsets. Breeders of pedigree cats usually supply a diet sheet and this should be carefully followed. Check whether your kitten has already been wormed and if it has had its first vaccination (at about nine weeks), make sure you have the vaccination certificate and know when the second injection is due. A pedigree cat should also have a certificate with details of its pedigree and should have been registered under an individual name at about five weeks old. The breeder will give you the necessary document to register the change of ownership.

Place the kitten gently in its carrier and put it on the back seat of the car, preferably with another member of the family sitting beside it, talking soothingly. Even if the kitten wails pathetically, do not be tempted to open the carrier or you may have a terrified little creature leaping round the car. If you are travelling on public transport, do not let strangers come too close or touch kittens which have not yet been vaccinated, or have only recently had their first injection.

Settling in

When you get your kitten home, open the lid of the carrier and allow it to come out in its own time. Confine it to one small room at first, making sure that there are no dangers and no open windows or chimneys. Let it explore and sniff everything in sight; stay with it and give plenty of reassurance. If it tries to go somewhere that is to be out of bounds, discourage it with a gentle hand but do not startle it with a reprimand yet. Within half an hour or so, offer a small meal of a favourite food. When the kitten has eaten, place it gently in the litter tray. You may need to repeat this once or twice at short intervals, and maybe scratch in the litter with your fingers to encourage it.

Some kittens will jump straight out of the carrier and begin sniffing round, coming back to you frequently for a rub and a stroke, then eat their meal and afterwards fall asleep in your lap. Others may go into hiding, huddle behind the carrier and not venture out for hours. When they do come out, they may not eat for the rest of the day; a nervous kitten may not eat for 24 hours or more. If this happens, don't panic. Make sure that its chosen refuge remains as peaceful as possible but go back frequently with quiet, soothing words. Stroke it gently but do not pull it out; wait until it is convinced that it is safe to emerge. Put down fresh food at every mealtime and take it up again an hour or so later, if it is not eaten. Make sure that there is a bowl of fresh water near the hiding place all the time.

You will have to decide, right from the beginning, whether you expect the kitten to stick to its own bed or share yours. Hygiene is one good reason for keeping cats out of your bed and getting a good night's sleep is another – your cat is unlikely to settle down for eight peaceful hours at a time and you will probably find yourself woken by tickling whiskers or a loud purring in your ear. Do not be tempted to let the new kitten share your bed 'just for the first few nights'. Your kitten will assume that this is where it is entitled to be and will make a great deal of fuss when you try to change its happy routine. If you intend to confine it to a single room at night, then start as you mean to go on. If the weather is cold, wrap up a hot water bottle (filled with *warm* water) and put it at one side of the kitten's bed. Some owners say that a clock with a strong tick, wrapped up in a corner of the bed, will comfort a nervous kitten, simulating its mother's heartbeat.

Introduction to other pets

If you take two kittens from different litters while they are under 12 weeks old, they are likely to get used to one another within a few hours, starting with some hissing and spitting and ending with a game. Introducing a kitten to an established family pet will take more time and patience. Sometimes the two pets, whether two cats or a dog and a cat, will become good friends, sleeping together at night and romping together in the day; sometimes you will not achieve more than a truce, with each pet going its own way and tolerating the other's presence when necessary.

A full-grown cat will accept a new kitchen more readily than an adult cat, who will be seen as a threat; it may help to rub the kitten with a piece of the older cat's bedding before they meet, so that it will smell familiar. At the beginning they should be fed separately and not left alone until all the early skirmishing and signs of aggression have disappeared. The older pet will need plenty of fuss and attention if it is not to feel left out and this is especially important if the established pet is a dog, as a resentful dog may wait its opportunity to attack the usurper. Dogs and cats are natural enemies but when they live in the same house, the cat will be accepted as a 'honorary dog' and some dogs can be very gentle and loving with a kitten. However, this will not happen in five minutes and the dog must be certain that its position in the family is unchanged. You may need to keep each animal in a separate room to begin with, except for carefully supervised meetings. If this takes several days, change over the rooms each day, so that they get used to one another's scent. For the first month or so, make sure that the kitten has a private bolthole – a box with a kitten-sized opening – where it can retreat if it feels threatened and the other pet cannot follow.

Introduction to children

Small children will be thrilled with the new kitten and may want to spend most of the day cuddling it but it is important to teach them that the kitten needs plenty of rest and should not be disturbed when it has settled down to sleep. You will also need to teach them how to handle a cat properly. Kittens are too delicate for rough handling and if they are grabbed hard or clasped tightly, they will probably fight to get free and scratch hard in the process. They will certainly remember the person who hurt them and may run away from the child in future.

Make sure that your child does not pick up a kitten by the scruff of the neck; only the mother cat knows how to do that without risking damage to the neck muscles. Picking it up with both hands under the front paws, so that the rest of the body hangs as a dead weight, is also bad handling. Show your child how to put one hand under the kitten's bottom, so that its back legs are supported, and the other under the front legs. Then the cat can be held in the crook of the child's arm, one hand supporting its rear and the other around its chest. This way it will feel both comfortable and secure. Few cats like being held like a baby, cradled in the arms with tummy upwards and if the kitten objects to this, it should be released immediately.

Kittens should be discouraged from rubbing round children's faces, because of the possibility of transmitting disease. Never leave a cat of any age alone with a sleeping baby. It may try to snuggle up to the baby's face, out of pure friendliness, and cause suffocation. Keep pets well away from a baby's meals – and a baby well away from a cat's meals! Most important of all, make sure that a baby or toddler does not touch the contents of the kitten's litter tray. As the kitten grows up, you may be able to put the tray out of the child's reach or, if you have a cat flap, put the cat's toilet facilities in a sheltered place out of doors. While you are still training a kitten, this will probably not be possible and it may be necessary to fit some type of baby gate across the doorway to the room containing the tray.

Visiting the vet

Your kitten should be vaccinated against feline infectious enteritis and cat 'flu, and the injections are given three or four weeks apart. If your kitten has not already been given its first injection before it leaves the breeder, you should arrange for this to be done when it is nine weeks old. If the first injection has already been given, make sure that the second is given on time. The vet will then give you a certificate of vaccination (which you will have to produce if you board your cat in a cattery) and this will act as a reminder for the booster in 12 months time. A good vet will be able to give the injection so skilfully that the kitten will not feel it and, though it may be drowsy afterwards, or may not be eager for its next meal, it should be itself again after a quiet rest.

This is a good opportunity to have your kitten checked over by the vet and to ask his advice on routine worming and, if you are not intending to breed, the age at which you should have it neutered.

Feeding

Kittens have very tiny stomachs, so they need small meals several times a day: four meals at regular times until they are 16–20 weeks old, then three until about 24 weeks and eventually just two. Cut out the second meal of the day by increasing the amount given at the first and third meals, then at about 24 weeks begin reducing the fourth meal, until it is left out altogether. Let your kitten's appetite be your guide as far as amounts are concerned. If your kitten comes to you at ten weeks, start off with a good heaped tablespoon at each meal. If you find that the kitten leaves a good portion of it, then reduce the amount; if it polishes it all off and looks around for more, then you are not giving it enough. Forking the food into little peaks will help your kitten to eat it; and the kitten's food is always served at room temperature, not straight from the fridge.

Milk is a valuable food for kittens but cow's milk may give them diarrhoea. They may be able to tolerate evaporated milk more easily; dilute it with two parts warm water to one part milk and serve it in small amounts after the first and fourth meals. However, cats quench their thirst with water, not milk, so you must ensure that fresh water is always available, even if you never see your cat drink.

Early training

Unless you take your kitten at a very young age, it will probably already have been trained by its mother to use a litter tray. Cats are basically very clean and if you put your kitten into the litter tray soon after each meal, it will soon get the idea. However, bewilderment and fright may lead to the occasional mistake. Keep an eye on the kitten at the beginning and if you see it squatting down in the wrong place, take it straight to the tray. If you spot the problem immediately after the kitten has made a mess, rebuke it sharply and put it into the tray. Never smack the kitten or rub its nose in the mess; it will not learn better ways but it may learn to be frightened of you. When you discover the mess some time later, there is nothing to do but clear it up as the kitten will have forgotten all about it and will not know why you are cross. Make sure that you have cleaned up thoroughly, as any remaining smell will encourage the kitten to use the same spot again. A rinse of white vinegar will usually do the trick, or the area can be with sprinkled with dry baking soda.

You need to make sure that your kitten knows the rules of the house from the beginning. If you let it do anything at all for the first couple of weeks, while it settles in, it will take you far longer to get the message across later. This means that every single time it does something that you do not want it to do, you should say 'no' very sternly and remove the kitten firmly from the problem area. If, for instance, it is scratching at the furniture, put it on its scratching post and make scratching movements with its paws as encouragement. Most mischief is caused by boredom, so you will minimize destructive behaviour by keeping your kitten busy and interested.

Going outside

It is wise to keep your kitten indoors until it is thoroughly familiar with its new home and has completed its vaccination programme. Then introduce the outside world gradually. For the first few times, go out with your kitten so that you can make sure that it does not get lost in long grass or chased up a tree by next door's cat. Choose a time when a meal is due, so that your kitten will come in willingly at the tap of its plate.

When you want your kitten to learn to relieve itself out of doors, begin by moving the litter tray gradually nearer and nearer to the door over a matter of days, then leave the door open and put the tray outside for a few hours at a time. Once your kitten is using the tray outside, begin putting some soiled litter in a suitable corner of the garden, to encourage the kitten to use this spot. Some owners continue to have a 'litter corner', to stop cats from scratching in the flowerbeds.

Collars and harnesses

If you want your cat to wear a collar (very useful for free-roaming cats, as you can fit it with a name and address tag) or walk on a harness later, you need to begin training while the kitten is quite young. A collar must have an elasticated section so that the kitten can slip out of it if it catches on anything. Fit it for the first time when the kitten is 3–4 months old and check each day to see that the collar is not rubbing the coat. Some owners like to put a bell on the collar, so that it is easier to find the kitten when it cannot be seen and to give the garden birds a better chance of escape before the cat pounces.

Some breeds, like Siamese and Burmese, take more readily to walking on a harness than others but if you do not want to allow your cat to roam free, it may be worth a try. You can begin training with an elasticated harness at about five months, leaving the harness on for about 10 minutes, then for longer periods. Keep an eye on your kitten while it is wearing the harness, as if it tries to gnaw through the elastic, its teeth may get caught. Elastic harnesses are good for initial training because they slip on and off easily, but once outside you will need to be careful, as your kitten can wriggle out of them. As your cat grows, a harness of nylon webbing or soft leather may be more reliable.

Once the kitten is accustomed to the harness, add a lead and let it trail that round for a short while. When you are ready to try an outing, let your kitten take its own time about going outside. Though there are some cats who will walk obediently alongside their owners like dogs, they are few and far between. Mostly, it is the owner who goes for a walk with the cat and so long as you are prepared to follow where it wants to go and not restrain it too much, you should both enjoy the outings. Never try to pull a cat after you or make it walk further than it wants to go.

Safety

Once you have a kitten in the house, you must remember to keep the doors of the washing machine, spin drier and refrigerator shut, so that it cannot hide away in a dangerous place. Keep the kitten out of the kitchen when you are cooking. It may not be able to jump onto high surfaces to begin with but it can certainly wind around your feet when you are cooking and cause an accident. It must be taught never to jump onto the cooker, as it can give itself a serious burn on a hotplate or upset boiling liquids. Never leave hot irons or kettles unattended.

Some types of house plants are poisonous to cats. If you have some treasured plants and it is not possible to keep them in a room that is out of bounds to pets, it is worth checking with the vet to see if they are safe. The harmful varieties include dieffenbachias, poinsettias, azaleas and most kinds of ivy.

Once your kitten starts going out of doors, read the labels on your plant sprays and lawn treatments carefully to check if they are harmful to pets. Cats can inhale toxic substances, absorb them through the skin or ingest them when grooming their paws. Never let your cat roll on a lawn recently treated with weedkiller and do not use slug pellets if your cat is likely to get hold of them. The creosote you use on the garden fence is dangerous to cats, so are paint, turps and paraffin. Anti-freeze is also poisonous to them and, unfortunately, they like the taste, so be sure to keep them out of the garage if there is likely to be a tempting little puddle that they might lap up.

Neutering

Male cats are neutered by castration, a very simple operation carried out under general anaesthetic. This can be done at any age from four months and your veterinary surgeon will advise on the right time: seven to nine months is usual. By this time the cat will have developed his masculine lines but not his objectionable male habits, like spraying the walls of your home.

For a female the operation is called spaying and involves the removal of the ovaries and the womb. An area of the cat's flank is shaved, a small incision is made and closed with two or three stitches, which will be removed ten days later. Spaying can take place at any age from four months and it is not necessary to allow the cat to have a litter of kittens before it is carried out. If a cat has already become pregnant the operation should be postponed, unless there are good medical reasons for it.

The veterinary surgeon will ask you to keep your pet off solid food and liquids for 12 hours before the operation and if you do not keep to this, you are risking your cat's safety. Most cats recover quickly and come home on the day of the operation, though some females may be kept at the surgery overnight. Some throw off the anaesthetic very fast but others may be woozy for the rest of the day, so confine them to a safe area and keep an eye on them. Males will probably be playing happily by the next morning but females will take a little longer and should be kept quiet for a day or so. Your cat will probably show no ill effects but watch for any excessive licking of the operation site, and signs of bleeding, or sickness and diarrhoea that might signal an infection.

3

Cat Care

Most routine care is straightforward common sense; cats do not need constant fussing or endless trips to the vet. They do need a good, balanced diet, proper grooming, sufficient exercise and plenty of affection. The good care you give your cat will show in its bright eyes, shining coat, curiosity and energy. If there is anything wrong with your cat its behaviour and appearance will change and a caring owner will know what signs to look for and when emergency action needs to be taken.

Diet

In the wild, a cat would eat the whole of its prey: meat, bones, skin and organs. This would give all the protein, fat, vitamins and minerals necessary for its survival. In feeding a pet cat, you will need to provide all these essentials, in the correct proportions. This is not as daunting as it sounds: a good quality cat food straight from the supermarket shelf is carefully formulated to give a balanced diet, though many owners prefer to provide a more varied menu. Changes of texture and smell add interest to meals and help teeth to stay healthy.

Adult cats usually do best on two meals a day. They need about 50 calories for each 454 grammes (1lb) of body weight, though this will vary a little according to the amount of exercise the cat takes. A mother cat feeding a litter of kittens will need 125–150 calories for each 450 grammes of her body weight. As a rough guide, the approximate calorie values of suitable foods

for cats are as in the following list:
Rabbit 600 calories per 454 grammes (1lb)
Chicken 500 calories per 454 grammes
Heart 550 calories per 454 grammes
Liver 600 calories per 454 grammes
Lean minced beef 750 calories per 454 grammes
White fish 500 calories per 454 grammes
Oily fish 750 calories per 454 grammes
Milk 400 calories per pint
Canned cat food 200 calories per small can
Dried cat food 1,600 calories per 454 grammes

Cats are natural predators and, as carnivores, they are not suited to a meatless diet, so it is unwise to try to make them live according to the principles of vegetarian or vegan owners. If you cannot bear to think of your pet licking its lips over meat or fish, whether served plain or disguised in proprietary foods, then it might be better to buy a goldfish.

Nutritional requirements

Proteins. Cats need far more protein in their diet than dogs. Suitable foods for providing protein are meat, fish, eggs, milk and cheese. At least one quarter of a neutered cat's diet should be made up of protein; for an unneutered cat it should be higher, at 35–40 per cent. If your cat cannot digest cow's milk, try diluted evaporated milk. Some cats get on better with yogurt which has a lower lactose content.

Fats. Fats provide concentrated forms of energy and should make up at least 15 per cent of the diet; 25–30 per cent is a good proportion for a young, growing cat. If you think that your pet's diet is low in fat, you can add a little pure vegetable oil to its meals.

Carbohydrates. These are found in starchy foods and can be used as bulk in your cat's diet. Add freshly cooked rice, crumbled brown bread or cereals. Carbohydrate is not essential for the well-being of the cat but can be a useful source of fibre for keeping bowels healthy.

Vitamins and minerals. Cats need plenty of vitamin A and about twice as much vitamin B as a dog of the same size. Their vitamin D requirement is low compared to that of dogs or people. Vitamin C is thought to be unnecessary, though convalescent cats seem to recover more quickly when fed with a vitamin C supplement. A balanced diet should give the vitamins and minerals your cat needs for good health so never feed them supplements without taking veterinary advice.

Proprietary foods

The proprietary brands of cat food on the supermarket shelves come in three types: canned, semi-moist and dried. The leading brands are carefully formulated so that they give a complete diet, containing everything that a cat requires to stay healthy. Cheap cat food is usually a poor buy, with a large proportion of jelly or filler, while the very expensive brands, in tiny pots, may make a tasty treat but are really designed to appeal to the preferences of the owner.

Canned foods. These are quite expensive, as you are buying a large proportion of water along with the meat or fish contents. The meat and vitamins are carefully balanced and there is a good variety of flavours.

Semi-moist foods. These are convenient to store and serve and, like canned food, they contain a good deal of water. They also contain preservatives, which can upset the digestion of some cats. Semi-moist foods may lack sufficient fat, so it is a good idea to add a little vegetable oil, butter or bacon fat. These are usually fed as part of a cat's diet, with perhaps one meal a day of canned food and the other semi-moist.

Dry foods. These are the least expensive, very convenient and easy to store and serve, and cats love the flavourful crunchies. However, they have been associated with urinary problems and it is important that a cat fed on dried food drinks a good deal of water. If your cat seems to drink very little, then only feed dry food as a snack, in addition to its basic diet.

A varied diet

If you keep your cat's diet as varied as possible it will not only keep healthy but will avoid fads that could lead to trouble later on. If you allow it to become hooked on one particular proprietary food and the line is discontinued or altered, you will have problems introducing a change of menu. Even if you serve only canned food, it is a good idea to rotate brands and flavours each day. There are pitfalls, too, in feeding fresh food. Carcass meat is low in calcium, vitamin A and iodine and a cat fed only on fresh meat may have weak bones in later life. Liver, a great favourite with many cats, can result in bony outgrowths round the joints which make movement painful.

Your cat will fare well if you feed a basic diet of proprietary food, plus one or two meals of fresh food a week. This could be raw or lightly cooked beef or lamb, cooked pork, rabbit, chicken or fish. Bones should be removed from fish and poultry, which should always be cooked. Meat must only be fed raw if it is fresh from the butcher and fit for human consumption (never feed meat from the knacker's yard). It is best to bake it in foil in the oven to preserve the juices, then mince or chop it into small pieces. If you prefer, you can add a spoonful of fresh food to the cat's first meal every day. Additional treats are grated cheese, cottage cheese or chopped, cooked egg – but in small quantities only – and 28 grammes (1oz) of lightly cooked liver once a week. For variety, add a little chopped carrot, cabbage or potato to meat meals. A handful of dried food each day, in addition to a mainly soft diet, helps to keep the teeth in good order.

Cats like routine, so try to feed meals at regular times each day. They are usually very good at regulating their food intake and are far less likely to become fat than dogs. There are some greedy cats but most will walk away from a dish containing their favourite food if they are not ready for a meal. If your cat regularly ignores one of its meals, or takes only a couple of mouthfuls before walking off, it may be that you are feeding too much and you should try cutting down a little. Most pets will enjoy a little of whatever their owners are eating but if you give them titbits while you are cooking, serving or eating your meal, you will encourage them to come begging, jumping on work surfaces or the table in search of goodies or winding themselves around your legs when you are carrying hot dishes. If you *never* give them extras outside meal times but add any treats to their regular food instead, they are far more likely to mind their own business while their owners have their meals and not develop habits that will annoy you later.

Stomach upsets

Most temporary upsets, diarrhoea or vomiting, will be due to unwise feeding, milk sensitivity or perhaps eating flying insects. If the cat passes a loose motion, take it off canned food and milk and feed it on white meat or white fish mixed with cooked rice for a couple of days. If the diarrhoea persists for an hour or two, withhold food for the rest of the day, then start the 'white' diet. In most cases this will put things right, but remember that diarrhoea can also be a symptom of serious disease so if the stools are bloody, if the cat is listless and dull or if it is vomiting as well, take it to the vet immediately. You should also consult your vet if diarrhoea persists for 48 hours.

Cats often vomit if they have eaten too much or too fast or if they have been chewing grass. If the vomiting stops within an hour or so, withhold food for several hours and then only feed a light meal. If that starts the cat vomiting again and the vomiting has already continued for several hours or the cat seems unwell in other ways, then take veterinary advice.

Drinking water

All cat care books tell you to keep a supply of fresh water for your cat at all times so it can be very galling when your pet sniffs disdainfully at the water bowl then goes off to drink from the birdbath or a dirty puddle. It is one of the facts of life that cats much prefer the smell of the suspect water outside to the smell of our chemically treated tap water and it may also object to traces of detergent left when you clean the bowl. Most owners notice that their cat will sniff the water as soon as it arrives but will normally not drink. Always be sure to rinse the cat's dish very thoroughly after washing, then allow the water to stand in it for a short time before you put it down for the cat.

Grooming

A longhaired cat needs grooming at least once, and preferably twice a day to keep its coat in good condition. Use grooming powder or talcum powder if the hair is tangled or greasy. Shorthaired cats need far less attention but a twice-weekly grooming session will get rid of dust and loose hairs.

Longhairs
Equipment: a bristle and wire brush; a comb with wide-set teeth on one side and close-set on the other; a wire rake or mitten for teasing out tangles; grooming powder.
Method: 1. Sprinkle the powder on the coat, then work it in with the fingers. If you massage the skin with your fingertips at the same time, it helps to loosen dead hair. Allow time for the powder to absorb grease and dirt.
2. Gently tease out knots or tangles with the rake or mitten. Use the rake or mitten carefully, making sure that it does not scratch the skin.
3. Once all tangles have been cleared, brush the coat thoroughly so that all traces of powder are removed.
4. Comb the entire coat from tail to head, working in gradual layers.
5. Brush and comb the tail, then shake it gently by the tip to separate the hairs.
6. Brush and comb the hair of the ruff forward to frame the face.

Shorthairs
Equipment: a soft natural bristle brush or rubber brush; a fine-toothed comb; grooming powder; chamois leather (or substitute nylon tights pulled over the brush).
Method: 1. Brush the cat lightly but thoroughly from head to

tail to remove dust and stimulate circulation, working with the lie of the hair.

2. If the coat is dirty, sprinkle on grooming powder, rub it in and allow it to absorb dirt and grease, then brush it out. If the coat is clean, omit this stage.

3. Comb the cat from head to tail to remove loose hairs.

4. Give the coat a final polish with a chamois leather. This will bring up the sheen of the coat and promote muscle tone.

Bathing

You do not need to bathe your pet as a matter of routine but there may be occasions when a free-roaming cat will come in looking as though it had rolled in raw sewage or helped a car mechanic to lubricate an engine and then you may need to take a hand. Light coloured cats may also need bathing before a show.

Wet baths. A double sink makes a good bath for a cat; otherwise you will need two washing up bowls. You will also need a shampoo specially formulated for cats, warm towels and a container for ladling water from one bowl to the other. Once you have groomed the cat to remove any burrs or tangles, half fill one bowl with warm water (test it with your elbow, just as you would when bathing a baby) and one-quarter fill the other. Stand the cat in the quarter-filled bowl and wet the coat thoroughly, then massage in the shampoo. Be careful to keep the shampoo well away from eyes, nose and ears but pay particular attention to the cat's underside, under the tail and between the toes and the pads.

Lift the cat while you pour away the dirty water, then stand it back in the empty bowl while you ladle water from the other bowl, rinsing away every trace of shampoo. Squeeze the excess water from the cat's coat with your hand, then wrap it in a warm towel, stand it in a warm place and rub it as dry as possible. Change to a dry towel and rub it again. It should be dried quickly to prevent chills. Some cats will allow you to dry them with a hair-drier; most are not that co-operative.

Dry baths. If your cat loathes getting wet, a bran bath may be less distressing for both of you. Use two handfuls of bran, heated in a baking tin until it feels comfortably hot but not hot enough to burn your hands. Tip it onto a spread newspaper, then add the cat and massage the bran into its coat. Use both hands, making sure that the bran gets right down to the roots, starting at the tail and working forwards. Once all the bran has been rubbed in, wrap the cat loosely in a warm towel and cuddle it for ten minutes or so. Remove the towel and put the cat back onto the newspaper, then brush out the bran, working carefully on a section of the coat at a time. You will be surprised how much dirt comes out along with the bran. Groom the cat next day and it should look and smell fresh and shining clean.

Care routine

Routine checks on your pet's appearance and health may save it from discomfort and catch any problems at an early stage.
Daily. Check for any evidence of bites and scratches that might need attention.
When petting your cat, check the coat for abnormalities and the paws for splinters, thorns or cracks on the pads.
As you clean the litter tray, make sure that the contents look normal.
Groom your cat as necessary.
Weekly. Examine the coat for evidence of parasites and look at the anal area to make sure that it is clean.
Check ears and mouth.
Fortnightly. Trim tips of claws, especially if your pet lives indoors. At the same time, check claws carefully; a broken claw may become infected if it is not treated.
Four to six-monthly. Treat for round worms and tape worms. Take the advice of your veterinary surgeon and ask him to prescribe suitable pills.

Ears

Any sign of greyish wax inside the ear should be wiped from the ear with cotton wool wrapped around the finger. For a cat with very hairy ears, you may need to use cotton wool slightly moistened with warm water and a smear of unscented baby soap to wipe away the wax but make sure that no water is allowed to trickle down into the ear. You should never poke around in the ear with cotton buds or apply any powder or drops unless prescribed by the vet.

If ear drops are prescribed (see pages 63–5 for more details on ear problems) you will need to put them well into the ear, then hold the cat for a minute or two while you massage its cheek, so that the drops have a chance to penetrate before the cat starts shaking its head. If the drops feel cold, your cat will automatically flinch away but if you warm the dropper in a dish of hot water, once the drops are inside it, they will be far more acceptable. Make sure that the dropper is dry, so that no water gets into the ear.

Teeth

Your cat should get used to having its teeth examined without fuss. The gums should look clean and healthy without any hard yellow or grey tartar deposits along the gum margins. Some raw meat or crunchy cat food in your pet's diet will help to clean teeth the natural way. Alternatively you can clean them with a child's soft toothbrush or soft wooden dental sticks impregnated with warm water or 3 per cent (10 volume) hydrogen peroxide, then a final rinse of salt water. However, you will have to begin when your cat is young and even then, some cats will always fight every step of the way.

Claws

Trimming your cat's claws regularly can be more comfortable for you and easier on your furnishings. It is essential if your cat is old or confined to the house. Unless your cat is very placid, this is a two-person job, with one of you holding the cat firmly, in a comfortable position where the light is good. Always use specially designed clippers rather than scissors, which can splinter the claw. Gently stroke and squeeze each paw to extend the claws, then you will be able to see the sensitive quick as a darker area within the white claw. Snip off the tip of the claw, keeping well clear of the quick and your cat will feel nothing.

Coat and skin

If you find any unexpected lumps or bumps or patches of bare skin, check with your vet. If your cat has been scratching, check for flea dirt, especially round the head and ears, the back of the neck and the root of the tail. A mild infestation can be difficult to identify, so stand your cat on white paper and brush its coat the wrong way. If tiny black bits drop out, dab them smartly with a damp tissue and, if they leave dark red smudges, then you can be certain that they are flea dirt and treat accordingly.

You can obtain good quality flea powder, specially formulated for use on cats, from any veterinary surgery, without having to take your cat for an appointment. Put a few pinches of powder on the cat's head and shoulders, keeping well clear of its mouth, eyes and ears, then rub it in, gradually working down the body. The rear and tail will need a few more pinches. Brush out the surplus powder. Some cats insist on washing out as much of the powder as possible right away and this may cause sickness. In this case, a spray might be more suitable but many cats are scared of sprays, as the hissing noise sounds like a predator.

Eyes

A cat's eyes can be cleaned with cotton wool buds moistened with warm water. Always wipe from the outer corner towards the nose. Sometimes cats have a sore eye because of a bump or a paw in the face while playing. If your cat's eye is obviously sore, examine it to make sure there is no foreign body, then bathe it with a saline solution: 1 teaspoon of salt in 0.6 litre (1 pint) of boiled water. If the soreness has not disappeared by the next day, consult your vet. You may then have to apply ointment to the eye: this is done by holding the cat's head firmly and applying the ointment to the lower lid. The eye should then be closed to spread the ointment and the surplus wiped away with a clean tissue.

Worming

Cats should be treated regularly for roundworms and tapeworms, especially if there are children in the household. Ask your vet to prescribe suitable treatment. Pills for roundworms can usually be mashed up into the cat's food but those for tapeworms are less palatable and you will need to put them directly into the cat's mouth.

To administer a pill, you will need a helper who can hold the cat's forelegs firmly, while supporting the rear end with the other hand. Then you take hold of the cat's head from above, holding it in the palm of your hand like a ball. Move the head up and slightly backwards, while you squeeze gently on both sides of the mouth with your fingers, so that it opens. Hold the pill between the thumb and first finger of the other hand, while you use the middle finger to press down the lower jaw. Drop the pill to the back of the tongue, then shut the cat's mouth and hold it shut while you stroke the cat's throat to encourage it to swallow. If the cat manages to spit out the pill and the coating becomes sticky, leave it to dry before you try again. Some cats seem convinced that you are intent on poisoning them and use all their strength and cunning to get rid of the unwanted pill. If this is the case, then use a little butter or liquid paraffin to grease the pill and wake the cat from its afternoon nap to administer it. You should find that the pill disappears before the cat realizes what is happening.

Beds
Most of the expensive beds sold for cats are designed to please the eye of the owners; your cat will not mind what its bed looks like, so long as it is warm and comfortable. You can continue to use a cardboard box, just as you did with your kitten (see page 26). Line with newspaper and some cosy material, discard each box as it becomes dirty and it will not cost you a penny. If you feel that a cardboard box will lower the tone of your home, you can buy the traditional wicker basket or one of the more practical plastic beds which can be cleaned and disinfected more easily. The various types of padded, fabric covered beds look attractive but they are far less hygienic. Some cats love bean-bags, where they can make a snug, body-shaped hollow that keeps them really warm; others seem to find the crackle of the filling intimidating. If your cat is suspicious of its beautiful

new bed, sprinkle a little dried catnip in it. You can buy this in a packet from the pet shop and cats love it.

Most cats like a warm spot in chilly weather, so a bed under a radiator or alongside the central heating boiler is usually popular. You can buy your pet its own version of an electric blanket, in the form of a thin metal panel, heated by electricity, which goes under your cat's blanket. Remember to put it at one side of the bed rather than in the middle, so that the cat can choose the warm or the cooler half of the bed. A night's heating only costs a few pence but if your cat likes to chew wires, you would be wise to buy a flex protector.

Litter tray

The litter tray should be placed in a quiet spot so that the cat is not constantly disturbed by comings and goings just as it is settling down to some serious business. Some cats like complete privacy and may require a tray with a cover over the top; you can buy one or improvise your own with a cardboard box with a hole cut in the front for access, placed over the top of the tray. Never put the tray near to the cat's food bowls.

Litter should be changed as often as you can afford it but providing you regularly remove all the solid lumps and faeces (at least twice a day and preferably after every use) and add a couple of scoops of fresh litter, you will probably only need to change the whole lot every three weeks or so. All cats are fastidious and will not use a dirty tray; some will refuse to use it a second time before it is cleaned and will use a corner of the kitchen or a nice clean piece of carpet instead, so if you have a fussy pet you will have to be vigilant.

The litter tray should be disinfected regularly, but you will need to choose a safe disinfectant as most of the ordinary household types are poisonous to cats. The most dangerous are those containing coal tar or wood tar or the chemicals derived from them, such as phenol (carbolic acid, found in many disinfectants used by humans, like TCP) cresols (found in Jeyes Fluid and many 'pine' disinfectants, though these are perfectly safe for dogs and people) and chloroxylenols (found in Dettol and similar products, quite safe for human babies).

Never use any disinfectant unless you are sure that it is approved for cats. Products marked under the names Shield and Roccal, the hospital disinfectant Savlon and the cattery owners' favourite Tcgo will not harm cats so long as they are used in accordance with the instructions given on the pack.

Cat flaps

Some cats always seem to be on the wrong side of the door and are experts at making you jump up to open it. If you prefer to make your pet independent of a doorman, a cat flap fitted in the outside door can save you a good deal of trouble and means that you can give your cat the freedom to come and go while you are out. Most pet shops offer a choice of cat flaps which should be fitted low enough for the cat to step through comfortably. A clear plastic flap is a good choice for a cautious cat, as cats do like to see what is ahead of them. Your cat will probably prefer a flap that opens both ways, so that it can come and go at will, but you can fit a flap that will only open to allow the cat to come inside. A lock or bolt is essential, so that you can keep your cat inside at night. The problem with cat flaps is that other cats can use them and if you find yourself with a kitchen-full of neighbourhood moggies, all fighting to steal your pet's food, you will need the type of flap that only opens in response to a device on your cat's collar, which is rather more expensive.

Your cat may use the flap immediately without any prompting, or you may have to use a little encouragement. At first, prop the flap open so that it can investigate thoroughly. At the next meal-time, let the cat see its food prepared, then put the cat outside and the dish of food just inside the flap. Open the flap a little, so that the cat can see and smell its food and it will soon come bustling through. Repeat the process at each meal, with the food first inside, then outside, until your cat is quite happy about the flap.

Indoor cats

Cats can live quite happily indoors, providing that they are used to this way of life from the beginning and they do not belong to one of the breeds renowned for its free-roaming ways.

An indoor cat will do better if it has another cat as a playmate, to keep it amused and exercised. A single cat will be far more dependent on its owner so you must make sure that it has plenty of company, fun and exercise. It will need a scratcher and some sort of climbing frame. It is not kind to keep a cat in solitary confinement while you go out to work for eight hours a day.

Cats like to nibble grass, which provides roughage and sometimes acts as an emetic, to clear some of the fur swallowed during washing. If they have no access to grass from the garden, you can buy a small pot from the pet shop and grow your own within a few days. It is unwise to buy ordinary grass seed to grow your own as it may have been treated in a way that is harmful to cats.

Elderly cats

As they get old, cats often sleep more, need less food and more liquid. Make sure they have a peaceful place to sleep, a good quality, light diet and more frequent changes of their water supply. A little vegetable oil or lard added to their diet can be beneficial. Sometimes an elderly cat may fare better on three or four small meals a day, just as it did as a kitten.

A six-monthly veterinary checkup is a good idea. In the meantime, pay special attention to ears, teeth and claws so that any problems can be sorted out. Old cats may not have the energy to groom themselves properly, so check the anal area, which may need sponging with warm water and drying. Make sure that an indoor tray or a cat flap is provided; the need may be urgent and your cat should not have to wait in discomfort until someone is ready to open the outside door. Never punish an old cat for an occasional mishap; instead put a sheet of plastic under a blanket in the cat's favourite sleeping spot or confine it to rooms where an accident is not a disaster.

Your cat needs plenty of love and affection in its declining years, even if it spends most of the time sitting quietly in a corner. Some owners import a new kitten at this stage but if your cat has always had the home to itself, this is not the right time to introduce a newcomer who will demand attention and probably irritate the old cat with its playful antics.

First aid

It is wise to keep a basic set of feline first-aid equipment handy and to learn what to do in case of an emergency – even though you hope it will never happen.

First-aid kit
- antiseptic, of a type recommended by the vet
- cotton bandages in several widths
- elastic bandage
- absorbent cotton wool
- cottonwool buds
- packet of small sterile dressings
- elastic adhesive tape
- curved scissors with round ends
- short-bladed pointed scissors
- square-tipped tweezers
- nail clippers
- eye dropper
- plastic disposable syringe
- rectal thermometer
- petroleum jelly
- liquid paraffin
- hydrogen peroxide
- antihistamine cream

Emergency action
Accidents. If your cat has been hurt in an accident, move it as little as possible and do not raise its head. Cover it with a warm blanket and, if the weather is cold, wrap up a hot water bottle (warm, not hot) and put it next to the cat while you wait for the vet. If you have to take the cat to the surgery, then use a towel as a stretcher, preferably held by two people. If possible, lay the cat in a box, so that it will not roll about with the motion of a car, and keep it warm. If you suspect a broken limb, do not attempt to apply splints unless you are skilled; you may do more harm than good.

Bleeding. A minor wound, with little bleeding, can be treated with antiseptic (make certain it is suitable for feline use) and providing it progresses well, no veterinary help may be necessary. For a more serious wound, take temporary measures, then take the cat to the vet as soon as possible. If a limb is bleeding profusely, tie a piece of cloth above the wound and twist a pencil in it, so that it stops the blood flow. Do not leave this for more than a few minutes at a time. If the wound is on the body, cover it with a pad (a sanitary towel may be suitable) and secure it with a crepe bandage.

Burns. Apply cold water or ice. If it is a chemical burn, use rubber gloves as you wash off the chemicals with plenty of water. A small burn may need no more than treatment with petroleum jelly but always consult your vet.

Choking. Wrap the cat in a towel, then push down its lower jaw. If you can see the object that is stuck in its mouth, you may be able to hook it out with tweezers, a spatula or the handle of a teaspoon. If you cannot dislodge it and you fear that the delay of reaching the veterinary surgery may be fatal, try swinging the cat gently by its hind legs with its head down.

Stings. On the paw, a sting will show as a hard swelling. Remove a bee sting and treat with a paste of bicarbonate of soda and water, or a weak solution of hydrogen peroxide. Wasp stings can be treated with vinegar. Any sting on the mouth or tongue needs veterinary attention.

Unconsciousness. If the cat's breathing is irregular or has stopped altogether, you should give mouth to mouth resuscitation. Check the mouth for foreign bodies or vomit. Once the airways are clear, place the cat on its side, hold the mouth closed, place your mouth over the nose and blow steadily into the nostrils for four seconds. Take a deep breath, then repeat and continue until you feel some resistance or the chest rises.

Travelling

When holidaying in this country, you may be able to choose whether or not to take your cat with you but remember that cats do like their own surroundings and become very confused if they find themselves somewhere strange. If you do take your cat along, make sure that it will be possible to confine it safely indoors for a time after arrival and that everyone will not be too busy to notice whether it is inside or out and to make sure that it does not wander off.

If you are holidaying abroad, you have no choice because all animals coming into Britain from abroad have to spend six months in quarantine. The regulations are strict because they are designed to prevent the introduction of rabies. Never let yourself be tempted into secreting your pet in a caravan or boat cabin. It is not worth the risk, as part of the penalty for breaking the regulations may be the destruction of your pet.

Car journeys

When you plan to travel with your cat it is important to let the cat get used to the carrier (for types of carrier, see page 25). Leave the carrier about with the door open, so that your cat can investigate and perhaps use it as a bed. If your cat is wary of it, try putting one of its meals inside and leave the door open while it is eating. Then try shutting the door for short periods, while the cat is sitting quietly inside.

Practise car travel with short journeys round the block. The noise and motion of the car may worry the cat at first but its wails will soon subside when it realizes that nothing unpleasant is about to happen. Never leave a cat loose in the car. If you have trained it to wear a harness and there is a passenger to hold the lead firmly at all times, then it may not need to stay confined in a carrier but remember that in case of an accident, a terrified pet may be able to escape.

It is better not to feed a cat for four hours or so before a journey, especially if it is prone to car sickness. On long journeys, take a litter tray and a water bowl with you, then you can stop every couple of hours and allow the cat to stretch its legs – but only while the car is closed and stationary.

Sending your cat by air

Cats usually travel in specially licensed, heated and pressurized holds in aircraft. They must be confined in carriers that meet certain specifications (check carefully with the chosen airline) and you will not be able to use your ordinary carrier. Let your cat get used to its airline kennel, just as you did with its ordinary carrier, so that when it comes to travel it will have its own smell all round it.

Cats should not be fed for six to eight hours before a flight and no food or water should be put inside the carrier; on long flights the airline will make arrangements for any necessary watering or feeding. Make sure that the cat has a warm, thick blanket to snuggle down in and arrange a thick layer of torn sheets of absorbent kitchen paper in a corner at the back, as a toilet area. You might try putting a few sheets in the litter tray for several days before the flight, so that your cat knows that this is the right place to use.

Each country has its own regulations on the import of animals and you will need to check with the embassy to make sure that you have all the necessary documentation.

Catteries

You may be lucky enough to find a neighbour who will come in twice a day while you are on holiday to feed your cat, change its water and litter and give it a little company. However, if you do not have someone who is totally reliable and who would know immediately if there was anything wrong with your cat, then you will need to leave your cat in a cattery.

There are one or two 'good cattery' guides on the market but they become out of date very quickly. Your vet will probably be able to recommend a well-run establishment, or you may get a recommendation from a friend but you should always inspect a cattery personally before booking in your cat. In most areas there is no shortage of catteries to choose from but they vary enormously in quality, so make a thorough inspection. Some larger catteries have a staff of helpers so the owner may not have the care of your pet; on the whole, the smaller cattery where the owner has daily contact with each cat is preferable. It is worth taking time to talk to the owner, so that you are certain that he or she really understands cats and cares about their wellbeing. Ask whether you can bring your cat's bedding and toys. Some cattery owners have strict rules and allow only one item along with each cat; you may prefer to avoid them. A caring cattery owner will know that your pet will settle far more happily with familiar things around it.

Many catteries have small timber sleeping houses with access to individual wired-in runs and these are probably the most hygienic. Infection can spread more easily in an indoor cattery, but these may be more suitable if you usually go on holiday in winter, so long as they have plenty of room and are well-ventilated. Look for the following signs of a well-designed, properly run cattery:

● The whole cattery should be spotlessly clean: houses, runs and the surrounding areas. There should be no unpleasant smells, even on a warm day, but no overpowering smell of disinfectant either.

● Sleeping houses should be large enough to take food and water bowls and a litter tray and to allow some room for exercise when the weather is bad.

● The sleeping compartment or pen should be light, well-ventilated and lined with easily cleaned material.

● Runs should be paved with smooth concrete; grass is difficult to cut and impossible to disinfect.

● The ideal is a 61cm (24inch) space between each pen but few catteries provide this. Make sure that good quality sneeze barriers are in place between the runs so that the cats cannot come into contact with one another.

● Beds should be fibreglass or clean cardboard boxes, not wood or wicker baskets.

● The surroundings should be fairly peaceful. If your cat is used to dogs, then a combined kennel and cattery may be suitable but otherwise, your pet may find the barking of nearby animals disturbing.

● The owner should ask you to bring the cat's vaccination certificate so that they can record the details. If you are not asked to do this, do not use the cattery.

● Pens should have an interesting view, rather than face a brick wall. Cats are great spectators and will be much happier if they can see other cats, animals in a field or passers-by on the pavement.

● There must be a safety porch or passage so that cats cannot escape when the door to their accommodation is opened.

● Accommodation must never be shared, even temporarily, by cats from different households.

Leave the phone number of your vet and also an emergency phone number, a friend or relative, for the owner to contact in case of problems. You should also note any particular food preferences, though it is surprising how cats lose their faddy eating habits in a cattery, where they suspect that other animals may come and steal their food.

Most doting owners worry about leaving their frightened looking pets in a cattery for the first time but, though you may feel you are shutting them up in a prison, cats feel secure in a small space and, once they know that the food will arrive regularly, they will settle in happily and even enjoy the change. It may be a good idea to have a short 'rehearsal' before the holiday, when you leave your pet in the chosen cattery for a weekend. It will then recognise the place and the people and know that all was well last time. It will settle in more quickly and you will not have to spend your holiday worrying.

4

Feline Ailments

Cats are tough, resilient creatures and your pet may go through the whole of its life without any serious problems. However, when illness does strike, it can do so with alarming rapidity. An alert owner can save a cat's life by spotting any changes in normal behaviour – refusal of food, excessive thirst, lethargy – and getting prompt veterinary help. Though experience will teach you how to deal with many minor ailments at home, you should never hesitate to consult your vet if you are in any doubt at all. He may be able to give advice over the phone and will certainly know when you should take your pet along for an examination.

The spread of diseases

Cat diseases may be either infectious or non-infectious, and infectious diseases may also be contagious or 'catching', whereas non-infectious diseases are not. The non-infectious diseases include those caused by the malfunction of certain organs, resulting in, for example, heart, kidney or liver disease.

Diseases may be transmitted in various ways. Viruses tend to spread through droplets sneezed or breathed out by an infected cat, which are then breathed in by the susceptible cat. Food, drink, bowls, or the cat's fur, may become contaminated directly, or through transmission by flies, with faeces, urine, vomit, pus or saliva from an infected cat, which are ingested by the susceptible cat, entering its stomach and bloodstream. Cats may eat disease-carrying insects, birds or small animals, or may be bitten by disease-carrying parasites. Direct contact between cats, without inhalation or ingestion, is responsible for the spread of some diseases.

From cats to humans

Zoonoses (pronounced zoo-oh-no-sees) are diseases which can pass from animals to humans, but luckily very few diseases pass to humans from cats. The most deadly zoonosis, rabies, occurs on the continents of America, Africa, Asia and Europe.

Ringworm is a fungal disease of cats readily transmitted to human contacts, and certain mites and fleas will pass from cats to humans. Bacteria from a cat may infect open wounds on humans, and scratches and cuts should be carefully cleaned and covered to avoid contact with the animal's breath, saliva or coat. Bites and scratches inflicted by cats on humans should also receive careful treatment, including a thorough cleansing of the wound and application of antiseptic.

Perhaps the most worrying zoonosis is toxoplasmosis, a disease caused by a microscopic single-celled organism or protozoan called *Toxoplasma*. This parasite can affect many animals, but only the cat spreads its infective cysts by voiding them in its faeces. The disease often produces no symptoms in the cat, but in a pregnant woman it may affect her unborn child by causing congenital defects. Humans can also contract the disease by eating or handling raw or undercooked meat. The normal way to prevent toxoplasmosis in the cat is to feed only heat-processed canned foods and well-cooked fresh meat, and not allow the cat to catch or eat wild prey. You should always wash your hands after handling raw meat in any case, and pregnant women should avoid changing the cat's toilet tray in case they pick up any germs from it.

Symptoms of illness

Generally speaking, an ailing cat loses its appetite, either partially or completely, and when this happens, the caring owner should always check for an obvious cause. Most cats eagerly wait their regular meals, and consume the entire contents of their dish within a few minutes. While a finicky cat may have slightly different feeding habits, there will still be a pattern, and any change in this should sound a danger bell in the owner's mind.

The incubation of an illness can also be indicated by changes in appearance and behaviour. The cat's coat may be held slightly erect, giving it an open or spiky look. The eyes may look rather dull, and the third eyelid may appear in the inner corner of each eye. The cat may seem to be thirsty but be reluctant to drink, crouching with its head over its water bowl, or it may drink copiously with gulping movements. It may go repeatedly into its toilet tray, but seem unable to pass urine or faeces, despite straining. It may resent handling and spit when touched, it may stop cleaning its fur and become odorous, and its breath may smell unpleasant. Other symptoms include sneezing, drooling, vomiting, diarrhoea and discharges from the eyes or nose.

The veterinarian will want to have accurate details of the onset and timing of any symptoms, to help him diagnose and treat the illness.

Temperature

It is useful to be able to take your cat's temperature, as this can be a very good indication of when to seek help. The normal temperature of an adult cat varies between 38 and 38.6°C (100.4 and 101.5°F) and it may rise one degree through excitement, fear or stress. A low body temperature should be treated with as much alarm as a high one, for a subnormal rectal temperature is indicative of some of the more serious feline diseases.

It is best to have someone to hold your cat when taking its temperature, and the animal should be lying or standing in a relaxed manner. You should have a special small-bulbed rectal thermometer in your cat's first-aid kit. Shake this sharply once or twice to lower the level of the mercury, lubricate the bulb with a little vegetable oil and insert it for one-third of its length into the cat's anus. Be firm but gentle, rotating the thermometer if necessary and aiming the tip in a line towards the cat's head.

Hold the instrument in place for at least one minute, remove it, wipe it with a tissue and read off the level.

Pulse

The pulse rate for an adult resting cat is between 110 and 120 beats per minutes. High on the inside of the cat's thigh the femoral artery passes close to the surface of the skin. If you place your middle finger lightly on the artery you should be able to feel the pulse. Count the beats for thirty seconds and then double this number to obtain the pulse rate per minute.

Taking samples of urine and faeces

To collect samples of your cat's urine or faeces prepare a clean, sterilized toilet tray. There must be no trace of disinfectant or detergent, so after washing and disinfecting rinse it copiously with cold running water and dry it with kitchen or toilet tissue. Place the tray in its normal place and put two or three small sheets of toilet tissue inside. Confine the cat, but otherwise treat it quite normally. It may be reluctant to use the sparsely furnished tray, but eventually will find it unavoidable. When the cat has urinated, pour the liquid into a clean glass jar ready to take to the veterinarian. Put fresh tissue in the tray, extra sheets this time, and the cat will more readily pass its faeces. This sample should be put in another glass jar or a small polythene bag for transportation.

Other tests

Other methods of diagnosing disease or injury may be used by the veterinary surgeon. X-rays of bones and organs are generally taken while the cat is immobilized under a general anaesthetic. Leukaemia and other illnesses may be detected by a blood test, a small sample being taken from a vein in the cat's foreleg and sent for laboratory analysis. Other diseases may be identified by examination of swabs taken from various parts of the cat's body.

External parasites

Fleas

Perhaps the most common of its external parasites is the cat flea (*Ctenocephalides felis*), which thrives and multiplies rapidly in warm, dry conditions. The adult flea feeds by biting the host and sucking its blood. Flea bites produce irritating reddish patches, which the cat may scratch quite vigorously, and around the bite may be found reddish grits, which are the flea's excreta. Some cats develop an allergy to the flea's saliva, and a serious and very common skin disease called flea eczema or flea allergy dermatitis may result from bites. In this condition, a wide band of skin along the cat's spine from the tail root to a point about halfway along the body is seen to be covered with numerous crusty pimples.

To treat a cat for fleas, a suitable proprietary brand of pesticide should be used exactly according to the instructions on the pack. The cat's coat should be groomed thoroughly to remove all dead fleas and excreta, and the debris burned. The cat's bedding and furnishings in the home should be sprayed with another preparation made specially for the purpose, which destroys the flea eggs and larvae. The cat should be removed while this is done to avoid a reaction to the toxic product. Special collars are sold for use on cats which are expressly designed to destroy fleas.

Mange mites

Eight-legged and microscopic, mange mites provoke a wide range of skin conditions in the cat, from a simple flaking of the skin resembling dandruff to a full-scale condition with large scaly patches, all collectively referred to as mange. Mange is extremely contagious and is transmitted by direct contact between cats or through grooming equipment. Some mange mites live in the coat, some on the skin surface and some within the skin. To treat the mange mite it must first be identified, and this is usually done by a microscopic examination of a portion of the affected skin. Each species of mite is treated with a specific pesticide and this, together with a knowledge of the mite's life cycle and strict attention to hygiene, generally results in its complete eradication.

The fur mite is found on dogs and rabbits as well as on cats. However, it is readily contracted by humans, and it appears as itchy areas on the hands, wrists and inside the forearms, and sometimes on the chest. If you develop such itchy areas, regular washing with soap and water kills the mites. You should comb the cat and check the combings with a powerful magnifying glass to see whether there are tiny moving mites. The cat should be shampooed once a week for three or four weeks using a selenium sulphide shampoo, rinsing thoroughly and drying completely before allowing the cat to self-groom. All bedding and furnishings should be cleaned, and dichlorvos fly strips hung in the rooms inhabited by the affected cat.

Harvest mites, *Trombicula*, live in decaying vegetable matter during their adult lives. As larvae, however, they are parasitic and appear as orange-red or yellow specks on the lightly furred regions of the cat's body, such as its ears, mouth and between the toes. The mite feeds by injecting saliva into the skin and then sucking the predigested blood. If left untreated, the cat may develop raw, bleeding patches and sores. This seasonal problem may be treated by washing the affected areas, drying thoroughly and then rubbing in a safe insecticidal powder.

Skin mites can be particularly troublesome, and the most common is probably the ear mange mite, *Otodectes cynotis*. It is thought that two out of every three cats harbour these ubiquitous parasites, which may live in small colonies within the ears causing very little trouble. However, under certain conditions they multiply rapidly, and the skin inside the ear reacts to the irritation of the mites' leg and body spines, producing a thick brown wax. As the mites breed inside the ear, dry, crusty material accumulates and, if neglected, may block the ear canal and cause other serious problems.

All cats should have regular weekly ear checks. If you suspect the presence of ear mites, have this verified by the veterinarian, who can look into the ear canal with an auriscope. If mites are present, a special preparation will be prescribed which must be used exactly as directed.

The head mange mite, *Notoedres*, causes notoedric mange, or feline scabies, a highly contagious and very debilitating disease, which sometimes affects whole litters of kittens as well as their mother. The mites are only spread by direct contact between cats, because they are fragile and unable to live off the host for more than a day or so. The minute female mange mite burrows into the cat's skin, making tunnels into which she lays her eggs. This action causes irritation, and wounds develop as the cat scratches and rubs the affected areas, generally the ears and the forehead over the eyes. Patches of hair fall out and the skin becomes scabby, thick and wrinkled into furrows. Bacterial infection can enter the opened skin and the cat may become seriously ill from blood-poisoning. In severe cases, the entire body is infected and the cat gives off a strange, mousy odour. The cat, and all other cats with which it may have been in contact, should be treated without delay under strict veterinary supervision.

Lice

Just as mange mites rarely attack cats in tiptop health, so the small wingless insects called lice are more commonly found on sickly cats. Only cat lice affect cats and there is no cross-infection between species. The parasite's entire life cycle is spent on the cat, and it is spread only by direct contact or infected equipment. The biting cat louse feeds on hair and skin debris, while the sucking louse feeds on blood. An infected cat is restless and scratches a great deal. It may sleep badly, lose its appetite and become increasingly agitated and depressed if left untreated. While the adult lice are fairly easy to kill, the eggs, known as nits, are individually cemented to the hairs and are resistant to sprays and powders. If possible, the cat should be bathed every ten days, and when it is thoroughly dry, a suitable insecticidal powder should be massaged into the coat and brushed through. A 'Derbac' comb, sold for use in treating human lice, is an effective way of removing some of the eggs, but in long-coated cats it may be necessary to clip away some of the fur and burn it to destroy the nits.

Maggots

Myiasis is a condition caused by fly larvae developing on or in the cat's skin. It most commonly occurs when for some reason, such as a debilitating disease, a cat has a heavily soiled anal region. Some flies may lay their eggs in the soiled and matted fur, while others lay eggs on organic matter on the ground, and when the cat lies on this, the larvae hatch and migrate into the animal's skin. To treat the cat, it is first necessary to clip away any matted or soiled fur, wash the area with soap and warm water and then remove the maggots one by one with blunt tweezers. After removing the maggots, apply a suitable antiseptic cream and leave the wounds to heal in the open air.

Ticks

Occasionally picked up by free-ranging cats, ticks are usually found on the ears, neck or between the toes, where they resemble blue-grey or brown warts. Sucking the cat's blood with their mouth-parts embedded in its skin, they rapidly swell from the size of a pinhead to about 1 centimetre ($\frac{1}{2}$ inch) in length. The fully engorged tick will then drop off the host. Free-ranging cats in a tick area should be regularly dusted with pyrethrum powder to keep these parasites at bay. To remove a tick it is necessary to first relax the mouthparts with a drop of surgical spirit before lifting it away with tweezers. If the tick is merely pulled off the cat's skin, the mouthparts will be left behind to fester and produce an abscess.

Non-parasitic skin diseases

Ringworm

Though few non-parasitic skin diseases strike cats, and those they do contract are rarely contagious, ringworm, perhaps the most serious of all their skin diseases, comes into this category. Despite its name this disease is not caused by a worm at all, but by a fungus, *Microsporum canis*. Highly contagious and quite difficult to eradicate, ringworm affects dogs and humans, especially young children, and so is a zoonosis. The fungus grows on the surface of the skin, in the keratin of the hairs and around the claws. Toxins pass into the surface layers of the skin and may produce itching and inflammation, hairs break off at the base of the shaft, and in classic cases circular lesions appear, most commonly on the head and ears or on the inside of the forepaws.

Ringworm is treated by applying an anti-fungus lotion to the areas over and around the lesions, and the affected cat is isolated and nursed on disposable bedding and with disposable litter trays and dishes. Everything from the cat's environment must be burned after use, and combings from the coat are also burned, with strict hygiene measures being followed at all times. Alternatively, the disease may be treated internally with the antibiotic griseofulvin, which is given in tablet form over a four- to six-week period. Though usually safe, the antibiotic must not be given to pregnant queens.

Dermatitis

The cat is subject to several sorts of dermatitis or eczema, in which the irritated skin may become dry and scaly or wet and weeping. Contact dermatitis is caused by substances such as detergents, cleaning materials, disinfectants and insecticides; allergic dermatitis is caused by the sensitivity to certain foods, or substances breathed in (such as fly sprays), or bites from parasites; while solar dermatitis is a reaction to the sun, most often encountered in white cats.

In all cases of dermatitis, the skin should be kept as clean and cool as possible, and every effort must be made to avoid the onset of extreme irritation, when the cat will scratch and inflict wounds that will become septic. The cat must be kept well fed and as fit as possible while the dermatitis is treated. Various creams can be applied to the skin or antibiotics, steroids and vitamins are available for internal treatment.

Stud tail

This condition affects entire males and females as well as neutered males. It occurs when the pores which secrete the products of the sebacous glands become blocked. It can be avoided by washing regularly around the greasy area at the base of the tail, using good-quality unscented soap. Afterwards, rinse and dry with talc.

Feline acne
This is found on the lips and chin, and very occasionally over the eyes of some cats. It is a similar condition to stud tail and should be treated in exactly the same way. Antibiotic treatment is occasionally required when a cat already debilitated by some other disease develops acne.

Hormonal eczema
Alopecia, or balding, occurs in some cats, notably neuters. The hair on the lower back and abdomen falls away leaving denuded areas or skin very thinly covered with fine and broken hairs. The cat rarely seems discomfited by the condition and there is no irritation. Synthetic sex hormones occasionally cause a regrowth of hair, and in some cases a change of diet with increased levels of vitamins in the B group has proved effective.

Internal parasites

Most of the cat's internal parasites are worms, including the long, cylindrical roundworms, the flat, ribbon-like tapeworms and the little leaf-like flukes.

Toxacara and *Toxacaris* species are thick, white roundworms up to 10 centimetres (4 inches) in length, and may be seen in the cat's faeces or vomited bile. The adult worms feed on digested food in the cat's intestine, and lay eggs which are passed in the cat's faeces. Larvae may be passed to kittens through their mother's milk, and the young creatures may become ill rapidly as the larvae migrate through the lungs to the intestine. An affected kitten may cough or develop pneumonia, but more commonly looks undernourished with a staring coat and a swollen belly. It has diarrhoea and may vomit up worms. Control measures are essential in breeding queens – dosing regularly before mating and then keeping the pregnant cat away from any possible source of re-infestation. Infected kittens can be treated under strict veterinary supervision from the age of three weeks.

Hookworms cause problems in hot, humid regions, and are small, hook-headed roundworms, which suck blood from the small arteries in the cat's intestinal walls, causing anaemia and weakness. Infestation can be controlled by carefully administered drugs, and re-infection is prevented by keeping the cat inside, with clean, dry bedding and litter.

Whipworm (*Trichuris*) and threadworm (*Strongyloides*) are present in the cat in some regions of the world. Their eggs are ingested from contact with contaminated faeces. The tiny worms live in the large intestine and may cause anaemia, diarrhoea and subsequent weight loss. Laboratory analysis of faecal samples can identify the worms, which are then easily eliminated by suitable medication.

The common cat tapeworm (*Dipylidium caninum*) may be taken in with ingested fleas and lice, and *Taenia taeniaeformis* with ingested intermediate hosts such as rats and mice. Both inhabit the cat's intestine, and live segments resembling animated, flattened grains of rice may be seen around the cat's anus and in its bedding. Heavily infested cats may be very restless or show some signs of gastritis; they eat a great deal but never seem to put on weight. Drugs to eliminate tapeworms are very strong, and should be given under veterinary supervision. A dramatic improvement in a cat's condition can usually be seen after a successful worming treatment.

Flukes are rarely found in cats, and are generally the result of eating raw, infected meat or fish.

Heartworms (*Dirofilaria immitis*) are slender roundworms found in cats as well as in their normal hosts, dogs, in many parts of the world. The microscopic larva is transmitted by the mosquito, being taken in with blood from one host and then undergoing some changes in the insect before being passed to another animal in the mosquito's bite.

Cats infected with heartworm appear relatively unaffected until the parasite has matured, when symptoms include breathing problems, fluid retention in various tissues and breathlessness after exertion. Treatment of the adult worms is very difficult.

Viral diseases

Feline panleukopenia (FPL) or feline infectious enteritis (FIE)

This highly contagious disease, with an incubation period of only two to nine days, is characterized by its sudden onset and quick succession to death. The disease primarily affects young cats. The affected cat appears depressed, refuses food and may vomit white froth or yellow bile. The temperature may rise to 40.5°C (105°F) at first and then rapidly descend until it is subnormal. The cat visibly dehydrates, sitting hunched and wretched, with its eyes glazed and its coat erect and staring. It may crouch over its water bowl but will not drink. If touched, the cat cries in pain, and the body feels rigid and cold. Death is normally rapid, but if the cat does survive for more than a few days, the condition shows itself when blood-stained diarrhoea is passed.

Early diagnosis and treatment are the cat's only hope of survival. Antibiotics to counteract secondary infections and warm fluids given intravenously by the veterinarian may stem the course of the disease, and constant and careful nursing is vital. During nursing, the cat must be meticulously confined to prevent any spread of the disease. All wastes must be burned and all equipment kept sterile. The usual period of quarantine for this condition is six calendar months from recovery date.

FPL or FIE is transmitted by airborne particles, on hands or clothes, or by fleas. Formaldehyde (formalin) is the only disinfectant known to kill the virus, and should be used with care. Vaccination is the only effective measure for the control of the disease.

Feline leukaemia virus (FeLV)

The virus is contagious, being transmitted by saliva, urine and faeces, but it cannot live for long outside the cat and, therefore, is easily killed by suitable disinfectants. It is not as contagious as other feline viruses, and is spread mainly by close contact over a period of time. It may also be passed from a pregnant queen to her kittens.

Symptoms associated with the virus are varied, and include anaemia, diarrhoea, vomiting, fever and laboured breathing. A blood test will confirm the presence of FeLV, but there is no cure, although temporary remissions have been experienced in some cases. In a confirmed case, it is usual to perform euthanasia.

Feline infectious peritonitis (FIP)
Peritonitis is inflammation of the peritoneum, or lining of the abdomen, and is a serious condition that can result from toxins and bacteria spread from wounds or ruptured organs. It can also result from a particular virus, which attacks several parts of the cat's body. It appears that many cats develop a natural immunity to FIP, and the virus is so fragile that it cannot live for long outside the cat and is easily destroyed by disinfectants. In large cat colonies it spreads rapidly, infected cats and symptomless cats carrying the disease, and kittens and cats under three years of age are most vulnerable.

Any sudden stress in a cat developing immunity to FIP may cause a sudden full and fatal peritonitis. The incubation period can be very long, possibly months, and the symptoms are loss of appetite, weight loss and a swollen abdomen. There may also be diarrhoea, vomiting, jaundice and anaemia. FIP does not always attack the abdomen, and may affect other parts of the body, including the central nervous system. In some cases the chest fills with the straw-coloured fluid indicative of this disease. Though measures to combat dehydration and inflammation ease the cat's discomfort, there is little chance of a cure, and most cats that contract the disease are put to sleep painlessly to avoid unnecessary and prolonged suffering.

Feline viral rhinotracheitis (FVR) and feline calicivirus (FCV)
Although a number of different viruses may be involved in the disease commonly termed cat 'flu, the most important are the FVR virus, which is of a similar form to that which causes sore throats in humans, and the FCV. In the United States, an organism midway between a virus and a bacterium, known as

Chlamydia psittaci, gives a 'flu referred to as pneumonitis, and this can be partially controlled by certain antibiotics.

FVR and FCV are relatively short-lived away from the cat, and their transmission is by direct contact or by airborne droplets sneezed or coughed out by an infected animal. Stress plays an important role in the spread of FVR, for cats which have recovered are often carriers, and stress stimulates the shedding of viruses in droplets. Stress may be induced by strange surroundings, for example a move to a new home, a visit to a boarding cattery, or a queen's visit to a stud. Some carriers, on the other hand, continuously shed virus.

FVR is the most common and severe of the cat's respiratory diseases, and is highly infectious, with an incubation period of two to ten days. The first symptoms include loss of appetite, general listlessness and sneezing. The temperature rises, the nostrils discharge, long ropes of saliva may hang from the lips and secondary infections may occur, producing conjunctivitis and broncho-pneumonia.

There are several strains of FCV, and a wide range of symptoms may be experienced, from a mild infection to a full and severe upper respiratory infection similar to FVR. Mouth ulceration is a typical symptom of FCV, and in some cases is the only symptom.

Antibiotics are administered to counteract the secondary effects of both FVR and FCV, and vitamins are given to counteract depression and stimulate the appetite. Affected cats should be isolated and carefully nursed. Very effective vaccines are available against FVR and FCV and may be combined with a kitten's vaccinations against FIE once weaning is completed, and then boosted by extra doses administered by the veterinary surgeon at prescribed intervals.

Diseases of the digestive system

The mouth
The mouth may become ulcerated during an upper respiratory infection, and this condition is also seen when the cat has nephritis. The ulcers appear as blisters, spots or circles on the

tongue, lips, gums and palate, and streams of saliva hang from the cat's mouth. The first symptom is loss of appetite, when the soreness of the mouth prevents the cat from eating. A veterinarian should be consulted to cure this ailment. Regular checking of the mouth is an essential part of cat care, and can prevent the build-up of tartar and the development of periodontal diseases. Gingivitis is an unpleasant condition in which the junction of the teeth and gums becomes inflamed and it should never be neglected. It may be associated with FCV, or it may be caused by injury, incorrect feeding or kidney disease. In severe cases, the teeth may have to be extracted and the mouth cleaned up. Antibiotics help to treat secondary infections, and multi-vitamins help to stimulate new cell growth. It may take a considerable time to cure, and even then the cat may have the characteristic thin red line along the gums. Cats should be fed a proportion of crunchy food from kittenhood to prevent the onset of tooth and gum diseases.

The stomach
Gastritis may be caused by a faulty diet or by the ingestion of toxic substances. Frothy white, yellow or blood-stained vomit heralds the onset of gastritis, and is soon followed by offensive diarrhoea. The cat must be kept very warm and quiet, and warm, boiled water may be given to counteract the often rapid dehydration until veterinary help is at hand. The cat may not eat for several days, but once the vomiting ceases, liquid foods may be given by syringe and vitamins by injection.

Colitis, or inflammation of the colon, is characterized by blood- and mucus-stained diarrhoea, and the cat must be confined in a warm bed until veterinary treatment is at hand.

Some cats become ill due to the presence of a hairball – a solid clump of hair formed from individual hairs swallowed by the cat during self-grooming. If the hairball cannot be passed in the normal way it will be vomited up, and may weaken the cat for a few days. Hairballs may be avoided by combing regularly and giving the cat a mild laxative during moulting.

Enteritis is inflammation of the intestines, and cats are prone to various forms of non-specific enteritis, which although not as serious as the fatal viral disease FIE, should nevertheless be treated with concern. The first signs of enteritis are a staring, open coat and diarrhoea, often yellow in colour and very liquid and offensive. Sometimes the stools may be dark brown and blood-stained. Giving plenty of liquids and keeping the cat as warm and quiet as possible may bring it back to normal the next day when the toxic agent has passed through the system. In some cases, however, vomiting begins and this is a signal to consult the veterinarian. In severe cases of enteritis the temperature drops, the cat dehydrates, the region around the anus becomes scaled and blistered by the liquid stools and secondary infections may set in. Such cats need dedicated nursing to restore them to full health, and for a small kitten, a severe non-specific enteritis may be very serious indeed.

Enteritis caused by salmonella bacteria occurs in cats fed raw poultry meat from unreliable sources. Heavy infestations of intestinal worms can cause enteritis in the young cat, and some kittens develop severe enteritis at weaning. Such kittens must be taken from their mother and fed carefully on hydrolyzed meat extracts and jellies, with special electrolytic solutions being syringe-fed to rebalance the body's fluids. When the appetite returns, binding foods such as hard-boiled egg white and steamed white fish should be offered for the first few days.

Diseases of the urogenital system

The kidneys
Poisoning, especially by phenols found in some disinfectants, causes acute nephritis in the cat, indicated by such symptoms as depression, loss of appetite, increased thirst, some vomiting, and the passing of very small amounts of highly concentrated urine. The cat sits hunched and cries when handled.

Chronic nephritis is encountered in old cats with malfunctioning kidneys. Such cats drink excessively, especially green or stagnant water, whenever possible. Large amounts of pale urine are passed, and the cat's breath is very offensive. Veterinary treatment can help nephritic cats, and special canned diets are available to aid the function of the kidneys.

The bladder

Bacterial infection may produce cystitis in cats, but most cases are due to the formation of tiny stones or calculi, within the bladder, which block the urethra. A cat with cystitis goes frequently to its toilet tray and strains but does not empty its bladder. This symptom must never be ignored, and urgent veterinary treatment is required to prevent rupture of the bladder.

The urethra

Urolithias means 'stones in the urinary tract', and the cat affected by this disease cries as he strains to pass water, and then licks persistently at the penis and prepuce. Veterinary treatment can remove the blockage, and the recovered cat is fed very carefully and encouraged to drink large quantities of fluid each day to prevent recurrence.

The ovaries

Queens may develop cystic ovaries, when they appear to be constantly in oestrus, though if mated never conceive. Such cats lose condition rapidly and are constantly under stress, and so should be spayed.

The uterus

Puerperal metritis can occur after kittening due to the retention of a dead kitten or a placenta. The affected cat will attempt to wash her genital region and then stop, turn away and give a plaintive cry. An offensive discharge will be seen on examination. Urgent veterinary treatment is required, for otherwise the milk supply will dramatically diminish, the kittens' navels may become infected, and the queen will become increasingly ill, vomit, dehydrate and possibly die.

In older queens, the condition known as pyometra may be encountered, in which pus forms in the uterus and the abdomen distends. The cat's temperature elevates, she is depressed and refuses to eat and she may vomit and will show excessive thirst. An emergency operation called an ovarohysterectomy is required to save the queen.

In queens held back from mating and allowed regular, persistent 'calls', endometritis, or inflammation of the uterine lining, may occur. The cat is listless with a raised temperature and spends a lot of time cleaning the genital area.

Caring for a sick cat

After serious infection, complete cleaning of the cat's accommodation with formaldehyde is often recommended. Formaldehyde is unpleasant to use, and great care is needed in its application. It is, however, very effective, especially in dealing with ringworm and other resistant diseases. Formalin is dilute formaldehyde, and 26 to 60 millilitres (1 to 2 fluid ounces) of commercial formalin, containing 40 per cent formaldehyde, should be added to 5 litres (1 gallon) of warm water. The formalin may be obtained from any large commercial chemist, or through your veterinarian. Sodium hypochlorite is much easier to obtain, more pleasant to use and is very effective indeed against feline disease. Commonly used for the sterilization of human babies' feeding bottles, and in commercial kitchens and dairies for cleansing equipment used in food preparation, sodium hypochlorite or bleach is marketed under names such as Milton, Domestos, Chloros, Delsanex, and so on. Directions for its use are printed on the containers. The strongest solutions must be used with care on bedding, carpeting and any absorbent surfaces, but can safely be applied to washable paintwork and floors covered with impervious materials such as vinyl sheeting or tiles. The strength advised for sterilizing feeding bottles is perfect for dealing with the cat's dishes and bowls. There is no need to rinse off the residual disinfectant before using equipment so treated.

Before using any disinfectant on a surface thoroughly remove all dirt and grease. If detergent is used for this purpose, it must be rinsed away before the disinfectant is used, as some disinfectants are neutralized by soap or detergent.

Nursing

Though expert veterinary treatment is an essential part of the sick cat's recovery, it is the quality of the home nursing that determines just how effective that recovery proves to be. The three essentials in successfully nursing a cat are:

maintaining its will to live;

providing adequate liquids and foods;

keeping the patient warm and clean.

Though each feline illness has its own needs and characteristics, nursing follows the same general pattern. The sick cat must be closely confined within a quiet environment that is easy to heat and clean. A spot-heater suspended over the bed can be adjusted to give the exact degree of warmth required, and the infra-red variety also provides a comforting glow, appreciated by most cats. The area must be covered with some easily cleaned material, and all the equipment should be suitable for sterilization by strong disinfectants or by heat. Disposable equipment should be used whenever possible. The nurse should have a supply of disposable pinafores just outside the sick room, a pair of slip-on shoes to don before entering, and a shallow footbath of disinfectant, changed daily. There should also be a holder containing a sack in which to place all materials to be removed from the sick room, including soiled equipment and pinafore. If no other cats are kept, or the patient is merely recovering from a severe accident or operation, then the above techniques of barrier nursing are not necessary. When other cats are kept and the illness is the result of a viral infection, barrier nursing is essential.

Nursing cats recovering from severe cat 'flu is time-consuming and often demoralizing. The patient may be so severely depressed that it seems quite ready to die. It may resent handling and fight against its food and drink. In severe cases ulceration of the mouth may cause pain whenever eating is attempted. The nostrils, eyelids and lips may be ulcerated and bleed when bathed, and diarrhoea and concentrated urine may scald the genital areas, which may also bleed when washed.

The cat must receive nourishment to live, as well as the antibiotics and vitamin injections administered by the veterinarian, and so if your pet will not eat, concentrated liquid foods must be gently syringed into its closed mouth. The tip of the plastic syringe is passed between the lips and side teeth, the cat's head is lifted slightly and the liquid is allowed to drip down the throat. Take care to prevent choking, and allow the cat to take a breath from time to time as its nostrils are probably blocked. Two tsp glucose to 1 cup water helps give energy.

After feeding, the cat must be cleaned. First bathe the eyes, lips and nostrils using separate swabs dipped in warm saline solution, containing 1 teaspoon of salt dissolved in 0.6 litre (1 pint) of water. Dry each area as it is cleaned, and apply a smear of petroleum jelly to the skin. Next lift the cat and place it gently on its toilet tray, stroking the back and sides encouragingly. Even very sick cats prefer to use their trays whenever possible. The genital areas must be washed with a little soft soap if very soiled, and then rinsed, dried and smeared with petroleum jelly. If the cat is constipated or the anus is very sore, a little of the jelly should be placed inside with the aid of a cottonwool bud. Soiled areas of the coat should be cleaned with talcum powder and gently brushed into place. Soiled hair should be clipped away and, unless the cat is very emaciated, the body gently massaged with a pad of warm cottonwool to stimulate the circulation and tone the muscles.

Incontinent cats should be nursed with disposable pads made from napkins or diapers, torn into shape and tucked around the hindquarters. Choose the type which allows only a one-way flow of liquid to prevent soreness developing and change frequently. Massaging the paws and legs often soothes and relaxes the sick cat. If it is unable to stand, place it on a different side each time it is attended to prevent pressure sores. As well as giving general care, tempt the cat with some strong-smelling food each day; potted herring, crab and lobster pastes are excellent for this purpose, and a tiny dab placed on the tongue often rekindles the cat's appetite. As its condition improves, move the cat's bed to the window, to stimulate its interest especially in the summer when the climate is warm.

Inhalation treatment
Inhalations help to clear the blocked nasal passages of the cat. First smear the animal's eyelids and nostrils with petroleum

jelly and then place it in a mesh container. Make up the inhalant, according to the directions, in a small bowl, and put this in a larger washing-up bowl placed on the floor. The mesh carrier containing the cat should be balanced neatly on the edges of the washing-up bowl, and a plastic sheet spread over the carrier. After ten minutes, the vapours breathed by the cat will have released streams of mucus from the nostrils which must be wiped away. Repeat this treatment as often as possible during the recovery period.

5

Understanding your Cat

A cat can be a cuddly, purring pet indoors then turn into an efficient hunter and a swift killer in the garden just a few minutes later. Understanding the make-up and the instincts of the cat can increase your enjoyment of your pet and help you to strengthen the bond between you; it can also help you to iron out the minor behaviour problems that mar your relationship.

The senses

Sight

The cat's eyes are large and very sensitive. They can adapt to a large range of light intensity, with the pupil dilating to a full circle to admit the greatest light under dim conditions and narrowing to a slit when the light is bright. This ability of the pupil to expand and contract means that the cat has excellent 'night vision'. Though it cannot see when there is no light at all, it has far better vision than its owners in semi-darkness. In dim conditions, light passes through the curved cornea and lens to strike the retina at the back of the eye. The light is then reflected by a layer of iridescent cells called the *tapetum lucidium* and this is what makes a cat's eyes glow yellow, red or green at night. The same glow appears in the flashlight photographs you take of your pet.

The cat's eyes face forwards and the fields of vision overlap, so that it can see everything in front of it, with no blind spots. This means that it can focus accurately on its prey and judge distances for pouncing and jumping very well. It also has an extensive peripheral vision field and quickly picks up movement to the side of the head.

It was once thought that the cat was colour-blind, seeing the whole world in shades of grey but the opinion of the experts has changed. Though cats do not seem to recognize colours in the same way as humans, many owners notice a preference for particular colours in toys, food bowls or bedding.

Hearing

To an animal designed as a hunter, acute hearing is as important as sharp eyesight. The cone shape of the ears helps to concentrate sound and the dozen or so muscles of the ear enable the cat to move its ears forwards and sideways, so that it can focus on the slightest sound and identify the direction of the scurrying mouse or fluttering bird. Any owner knows that a cat can distinguish the sound of its own dish from the rest of the family crockery or the click of the cupboard door in which the tins of cat food are kept from all the other kitchen noises.

Cats can hear sounds around two octaves higher than their owners and about half an octave higher than a dog's ears can register. In old age, some cats do become deaf and this can be very dangerous if they live in an area with busy traffic. Deafness can also be hereditary, particularly among white cats with blue eyes, and should be considered when you are choosing a cat.

Smell

The cat's olfactory region is far larger than would normally be expected in an animal of its size, so it is not surprising that the sense of smell is highly developed. In a new-born kitten, smell is the predominant sense and it is vital for the survival of the cat in the wild, helping it to locate food and identify danger. Your domestic cat will investigate anything that arrives in its home by sniffing; when you return from an outing, its nose will tell it a great deal about where you have been and what other animals you have met. You will usually find that your pet enjoys the first meal out of a can best, as the smell is strongest when first opened and it is more sensitive to tainted food than humans.

Cats have a sense that humans do not share: a small pouch lined with receptor cells in the roof of their mouth, called the Jacobson's organ. When you see your cat making a strange grimace, with its lip curling like an aristocratic lady showing disapproval, it is transferring a particular scent – interesting sexual smells in particular – to the Jacobson's organ for identification. The grimace is called 'flehming' and is often seen when a cat scents catnip (*nepeta cataria*). You will be doing your pet a favour if you grow the plant in your garden. Not all cats respond to it but those who do seem to go into an ecstatic trance, rolling blissfully. Dried catnip is often used in toys and if you sprinkle a little on a plate for them to snuffle in, they will often begin to gambol like kittens.

Taste

The cat is not thought to have a highly developed sense of taste, with smell and texture playing a large part in their enjoyment of particular foods. It is sometimes said that cats do not respond to sweet tastes but some owners find that their cats love a taste of Christmas cake and fight for a share of a sugary doughnut, so their reactions to sweet tastes do seem to vary.

The cat uses its tongue like a spoon, enabling it to lap liquids and it usually laps several times to fill its mouth before swallowing. The taste buds are carried by mushroom-shaped papillae along the front and side edges of the tongue; they are not carried by the papillae along the centre of the tongue. These central papillae give the tongue its rough feel and are used for rasping food from the carcass of its prey and also for grooming.

Sixth sense

Many people believe that cats possess some sense that humans have never had or have lost. Many of the special abilities that cats apparently demonstrate can be explained away. The cat that runs to the door several minutes before its owner arrives home may have heard the unmistakable footsteps long before we could hear them; the cat that seems to sense when it is Friday may be responding to small changes in household routine, scarcely noticed by its owner.

However, some cats have shown an amazing ability to find their way back to an old home or to rejoin a family that has moved house, often travelling hundreds of miles, crossing mountains and rivers to get there. Sceptics dismiss this, saying that fond owners are only too ready to imagine that the black cat that has appeared on the doorstep of the old or new home is dear old Sylvester, when it is really a different cat. However, there are several well-researched instances that seem to prove a 'trailing' ability. A cat that followed its former owners from California to Oklahoma had a particular bone deformity that identified it beyond doubt. Another cat, turning up to greet a family in California, after being left at its previous home in New York, was identified because a bite injury had left it with an injury to the tail vertebrae, unlikely to be duplicated in an identical looking cat.

Cat talk

Cats express their feelings very clearly, communicating with their voices, their bodies, their tails, eyes and ears. The more time you spend with your pet, the better you will understand the subtle ways in which it conveys its mood and its wants.

Voice. Cats have a large vocal range, though some are more ready to be 'chatty' than others. Mother cats use a sort of 'chirrup' sound when talking to their kittens and many adult cats use this as a greeting to their human owners. The mother cat uses many other sounds in talking to her kittens. When she wants them to follow her, she encourages them with a soft 'prrrrp'. She uses gentle growls and mews to scold them and when she wants them to come to feed, she gives a cry similar to her calling cry in oestrus, though far softer.

Cat to cat language includes the full-throated, penetrating cry of the queen on heat and a whole repertoire of sexual language during mating. When cornered and scared, a cat will hiss and yowl and when it is threatening a feline intruder it may utter a deep, throaty wail, as a clear warning that it will attack if provoked. When watching a bird through the window, it will make excited little clicking sounds, as though it was chatting to itself about the treat in store.

Though a kitten's voice is fully developed at three months, it will add sounds and intonations long after that and the range of your pet's communication will depend to some extent on how much you talk to it and stimulate it to respond. Your pet will develop its own subtleties of the miaow, so that you can tell if it is begging for food, complaining about lack of attention or telling you that it is anxious or cross. Growls also come in a good range, from a scream of fear to a choking rasp of fury.

Purring is usually a sign of happiness, either the contentment that comes from stroking or curling up on its owner's lap or the pleasant anticipation of a treat or a game. As a phenomenon, purring has never been properly explained; it may be voluntary or involuntary. All cats purr, though some purrs are so loud that they fill the room and others so soft that you simply feel the purr as vibration. Kittens begin to purr as early as one week of age as they nurse and this may be a sign to the mother to release milk, as they will not purr in response to petting at this age. An adult cat will often knead its owner's lap with its paws, stretching and contracting its toes, just as it kneads its mother's nipples to increase the food supply. Frequently cats will purr when they are in pain and you may notice that, if your cat is ill and you have to carry out some unpleasant form of treatment, your cat will purr all the time. In this case, it seems that purring is a signal that the cat is harmless and submissive, so that it is telling the world that all it wants is to be left alone.

Tail. The signals given by the tail can be just as important as vocal communication. When a cat comes towards you with its tail held straight up in the air, it is offering a friendly greeting. When the tail is held up in the air with the tip crooked, the cat is friendly and interested but still has slight reservations. When the tail is sticking straight out behind, something exciting is going on – the cat may be in the middle of a hunting trip or on its way back from a successful foray, feeling pleased with itself. Many people believe that a twitching tail means irritation but it is more likely to mean curiosity or indecision. If a cat that has been sitting happily on your lap starts twitching its tail, it is probably thinking about leaving and is torn between staying in this warm, comfortable spot and going in search of more interesting pastimes. When the tail lashes from side to side, it can mean anger or aggression.

The cat is showing fear when it wraps its tail downwards between its legs but if it curls downwards, then up again at the tip, it is likely to be feeling at peace with the world. A really angry cat will hold its tail straight out behind with all its hairs standing up, then just before launching into the attack it will bend the tail over and perhaps slightly to one side.

Eyes. These also act as a barometer for a cat's moods. When strangers are about, its eyes will be fully open and watchful; once it relaxes and begins to trust the new person, they will be half closed. The pupils of the eye always expand in interest or anticipation: when food is on the way or it sees the prospect of a game. When the cat is frightened, the pupils are widely dilated and this can mean that it is about to fight or to flee.

Ears. An angry cat, which may be preparing to attack, holds its ears back and close to the head, so approach with care. If the ears are on their way back, take it as a warning that the cat is displeased about the way things are going. When it is alert and watchful, its ears will be pricked and forward. If you talk to your cat and see its ears flick, even while it seems to ignore you, it is telling you that it hears you perfectly well but does not choose to answer.

Predatory behaviour

Cats are designed to catch and kill successfully and they start to rehearse their hunting skills when they are only a few weeks old, crouching to ambush one another and pouncing with glee. Even a well-fed domesticated cat will still hunt for sport with mice and birds both fair game, and flies, grasshoppers and even wasps give them plenty of practice in stalking and chasing. Owners who keep a cat as a mouser often think that it will perform better if it is under-fed but in reality, hunting cats are more efficient if they are well-fed and in good condition.

The cat usually hunts alone and will have its own favourite ambush spots and stalking areas. It is a patient hunter, waiting motionless for hours when necessary, then approaching its prey stealthily on soft paw pads with retracted claws. Once it is within reasonable striking distance, it flattens its body to the ground, gliding along with head outstretched and ears forward to pick up the slightest sound. When it senses that the time is right, it builds up momentum by swinging its hips and tail, then it catapults forward, its powerful hindquarters providing propulsion. It grips its prey in its front paws, with claws fully extended and, if it is hungry, it will kill with a quick neck bite.

When a cat eats its prey, it will probably begin with the head and eat the whole carcass. Indigestible parts like fur and feathers may be vomited back later. When cats regularly eat fresh prey, they may not need to drink because the carcass has such a high fluid content. A well-fed cat will probably not eat its prey and may play with it for some time before killing it. It will be very excited by the chase and catch and may toss the captured creature around for an hour or more, diving and leaping on it, seeming to forget it and then leaping on it again with fresh enthusiasm the moment it moves. This has nothing to do with cruelty; it is simply that the cat's hunting instinct responds to anything that moves. It is useless to try to distract the cat or pull it away, as it is in a state of high excitement.

As cat-lovers are often bird-lovers too, owners may be upset when they find a dead bird laid out as a present on the doorstep or, even worse, on the dining table. However, smacking or reproving your pet for following its natural instincts is unfair. Your cat will be confused rather than deterred to find its gift rejected so vigorously. Make sure that you do not put out food in your garden for the birds, as this is only tempting them into danger and giving your cat ready-made targets. If it becomes a real problem, you might try a type of aversion therapy, which entails making a realistic looking 'bird', covered with feathers and dangling it from the end of a stick on a piece of string. Fill one of the plastic bottles sold to spray plants with fungicide (keep it for the cat only) with water and, every time the cat tries to attack the 'bird', spray it with water. Many owners have found this very effective but remember that, if your cat was ever lost for a few weeks – which can happen to the best-loved pet – it might need all its hunting skills to survive.

Territorial behaviour

Territory is very important to a cat, though the size of the territory may depend on how many other cats live in the neighbourhood. It may be as small as a couple of metres outside the back door or extend to several blocks and an unneutered male may control several hectares. The territory will be defended against intruders and, though cats do wander into one another's territories, they usually do so with care, avoiding confrontation. Newcomers, moving with their family into a house where no cat has lived before, will have a hard time establishing themselves, as they are moving into territory controlled by next door's cat and one or other will have to learn to back down.

The most obvious way of marking territory is by spraying. A tom cat will mark his territorial boundaries by spraying urine on his chosen spots regularly. Some neutered cats also spray, though their urine does not have the strong, distinctive smell of the male. Marking is also performed by head and tail rubbing. Cats have scent glands above the eyes on either side of the forehead and along the lips and others near the root of the tail. You will see your cat rubbing its head on objects, both inside and out and even standing on its hindlegs to press its face harder and imprint its scent more firmly. This may be followed by rubbing the whole length of the body and then winding the tail around the area to be marked. When your cat rubs itself around your legs in friendly greeting it is really proclaiming that you are its personal property.

Territories are patrolled on set pathways and you may find that your lawn has a definite track running across it at a territorial boundary. If your cat has been away from home, the first thing it will do on its return is to check and remark the boundaries. If you have more than one cat, they will usually hold territory jointly but you may find that one decides that a particular armchair or spot on the fence, or even your bed, is its own special place and out of bounds to the others.

Most of the time, cats will sort out their territorial disputes without fighting. They may square up to one another, glaring, arching their backs and fluffing out their coats and tails to make themselves look bigger and more formidable. They then walk around one another, legs stiff, staring one another in the face the whole time. The whole thing may end with one cat capitulating, looking away and shutting its eyes. It may then slink off, trying to look as though it was not losing face. If neither will back down, which is more likely with unneutered males, they may fight. The second stage in the threat display begins when both cats begin to growl and they may start salivating as they circle one another. The attack comes suddenly with one cat leaping for the enemy's throat, biting hard and raking at the other cat's body with its back feet. The cats roll over and over, locked together as they bite and scratch. The fight is usually brief but it can be bloody, with lumps of cat flying in all directions. At the end the winner may bite the loser at the base of the tail or mount it, as though mating, as a gesture of victory. Most fights look worse than they are but they can result in quite severe injury. If you know that your cat has been involved in a bitter fight, check it over carefully, as an untended bite can result in a painful abscess that may need surgery.

Sexual behaviour

Female cats are at their most fertile between the ages of two and eight and males between two and seven, though they may go on breeding all through their lives. In natural conditions the weather influences the female's sexual cycle, which is at its peak in March and April, then again between June and September. Cats kept indoors in artificial heat and light can breed at any season of the year.

It is easy enough to recognize when the female is about to be on heat and oestrus has four distinct stages:
1. *Pro-oestrus*. The cat is extra affectionate but also restless, pacing around the house and rubbing her scent glands against the furniture.
2. *Oestrus*. This lasts about seven days. The cat is agitated, often rolling on the floor and perhaps refusing to eat. She will probably yowl loudly and persistently, to the point where non-

cat owning neighbours may think you are ill-treating her. During this time she will be very receptive to the advances of a male and if you stroke her along the spine, she takes up the mating position, crouching with her hindquarters raised and her tail bent stiffly to one side. Extra care must be taken because she may try every way she knows to escape from the house.

3. *Metoestrus.* If the cat is not mated, the reproductive system begins to relax. This stage lasts for 24 hours and though she may still accept the advances of a male during this time, she may be reluctant to allow actual mating.

4. *Anoestrus.* This is the resting period when the female leads a peaceful life, without interest in males. It can vary in length from 10 days to several months. Oriental cats call more often than other breeds and some owners say that they always seem to be either 'calling', pregnant or nursing.

The male can mate at any time and is attracted to the female by her strong scent and her 'call', which he seems to be able to hear from several kilometres away. Once the male and female are together, the queen's posturing and rolling excites the male and he will be eager to mount her, though she may go through a ritual of spitting and clawing before she allows it. Among pedigree cats, the mating process is carefully controlled but in the wild several males may be attracted to one queen and fights may break out to decide which cat will mate her. She may mate with the same male several times or with several different males.

The queen will crouch with her rear offered to the male, her tail swung to one side. The male, after circling her and perhaps attempting to sniff at her rear end, jumps on her from behind, grabbing the loose skin at the back of her neck with his jaws. He pauses briefly to test her reaction then places one foreleg on either side of her shoulders and treads alternately on her haunches with his back paws, persuading her to lift her rump. A receptive female begins to tread with her own hindlegs but an unwilling female will squirm out of the male's grip and run away. Once the female is settled in the correct position, the male curves his back into an arc and penetrates her. The actual mating is a brief affair, with ejaculation taking place after a few seconds of rhythmic thrusting of the male's hips.

The withdrawal is usually accompanied by a howl from the female, which is thought to be a cry of pain caused by the barbs on the male's penis, and the male jumps hastily away as the female swipes at him with claws outstretched. She may pursue him briefly, spitting and hissing, before she begins to roll vigorously on the floor, pushing herself along with outstretched limbs. After a moment or two, both cats begin to clean their genital areas and before long will both be ready and willing to mate again.

Sleeping

Cats are designed to use their energy in short spells, long enough to catch sufficient food in the wild. The remainder of the time they spend relaxing, napping or sleeping. They have two types of sleep: very light sleep, seen in the 'cat-naps' they take throughout the day, when their blood pressure remains normal, their temperature drops slightly and their muscles never completely relax, and deep sleep when their temperature rises, their blood pressure falls and their muscles relax. Kittens sleep a good deal of the time and sufficient sleep is important to their development. They will often fall asleep in the middle of a game, in a tangle of arms and legs and they should be left alone until they are ready to play again. Adult cats spend about 16 hours out of 24 sleeping and about one third of this is deep sleep. Though they can sleep in any position – with their heads hanging over the side of a chair, with another cat draped across them or perched on a narrow fence top – they need peace and security for deep sleep. Tests have shown that if cats are in a state of anxiety for some time, so that they miss out on their deep sleep, their heart beats speed up and they are more prone to illness.

When cats are in a deep sleep phase they often dream, with whiskers and tail twitching, tongue flicking, their paws making running movements. At the same time they may make growling or purring noises. Of course, no one knows what cats dream but it certainly looks as though they are reliving their day's hunting trips or dreaming about the fat bird that got away. Even when it is in deep sleep, the cat's hearing remains acute, as a defence mechanism, and any unusual noise can rouse it immediately.

Movement

Cats are designed so that their movements at all speeds are graceful and fluid. They walk in 'four time' – right foreleg followed by left hindleg, then left foreleg followed by right hindleg – and this results in an even, flowing gait. They can produce a burst of speed when necessary but cannot maintain this for a long time. The gallop, used when the cat flees from danger or when it rushes to secure its prey, consists of a series of long, low leaps.

Jumping

A cat can jump four or five times its own height from a still, crouching position. It will take its time, judging the height by eye, then tensing the hindquarters before leaping forwards and upwards, landing with enough room for an accurate landing by the hindlegs, with the forelegs used to correct balance if necessary. Climbing down is always more tricky because it will land first on its forelegs, which can be badly jarred if the height is too great. You will see your pet weighing up the descent, edging forward with its head and shoulders as far down as possible before it pushes off with its hindlegs.

Climbing and balance

Kittens practice by climbing curtains and adult cats climb trees for fun as well as to get out of trouble and to spit at their tormentors from a safe height. The extended claws, to grasp and grip, and the strong muscles along the back and in the legs make it possible for the cat to haul itself up a vertical surface. It can then balance on the top of a fence or run along a narrow branch, using its tail to help distribute its weight.

As with jumping, coming down is harder. The cat's claws

point in the wrong direction for making a headlong descent so it usually comes down backwards, lowering itself in short drops until it is near enough to the ground to make a turning jump and land on its feet. Sometimes a cat will climb too high, especially if it is being chased, and will cry pitifully to tell you that it is stuck. Providing the cat is safe, it is wise to leave it for a time, as it may nerve itself to climb down and it should be given every opportunity to do so. However, a rescue by ladder is sometimes necessary.

The cat is well known for its astonishing self-righting ability, which means that it can land on all four feet when falling from a height, no matter what angle its body was in at the start of the fall. However, this does not mean that a cat is never hurt in a fall; it may end up with fractures or split the hard palate in the mouth as it hits its chin on the ground.

Washing

Most cats are fastidious and wash diligently, though some do allow their coats to get quite grubby before cleaning themselves. The action of light and warmth on the cat's coat seems to stimulate the washing reflex and the whole cleaning ritual often begins after a nap in the sun. The paw and the tongue, covered in tiny papillae which act as brush and comb, are used for washing: the cat licks its paw thoroughly, then passes the paw over its face and head, round its ears, across the eyes and down the cheek to the chin. The other paw repeats the process on the other side of the head. Each shoulder and foreleg is licked and groomed in turn, then the flanks, the genital area, the hindlegs and finally the tail from root to tip. Teeth may be used to pull out tangles and bits of dirt from between the toes.

Some cats wash carefully after being stroked, presumably to remove all human smell from their coats. Washing is also soothing and you may see your cat begin to groom itself immediately after it has had a fright or feels that its dignity has been impaired. The very action of grooming seems to restore its self-esteem. When cats from the same household groom one another, it is a sign of great affection. If one cat is more nervous than the other, you may see the placid cat licking the other to calm it at times of stress.

Bad habits

There is a widespread idea that cats are untrainable but this is very far from the truth. Unlike dogs, cats have no overwhelming desire to please their owners, so are not likely to jump around performing tricks, but they can be taught that certain actions are in their best interest and others bring unpleasant consequences. It is essential that you, as the owner, are the boss in your household. Most cats readily accept a hierachy, with you as the chief, but it means that you must act to stop bad habits before they become a regular part of your cat's life and are far more difficult to break. The first step is to try to understand why your cat is using the corner of the living room as a lavatory or ripping your settee to bits; you may be able to solve the problem by moving the litter tray or investing in a new scratching post. If none of your measures work, you will need to rely on consistent discipline or aversion therapy.

Scratching

This is probably the most frequent problem: your cat rakes its claws down the side of your chairs or rips your wallpaper from the walls. If you have no scratching post, make or buy one. If your cat ignores the post in favour of your furniture, make sure that the post is stable, so that it does not rock when attacked by the cat and that it is long enough to allow your cat to stretch its full length as it claws. Try attaching a toy with a bell at the top of the post; sprinkle catnip if it is covered with carpet or sew a mouse-shape, stuffed with dried catnip, and tie that on the post.

Every time you see your cat extending a paw to scratch at the furniture, say 'No' very firmly and throw a rolled up newspaper to land as close as possible. You must do this every single time, if your cat is to get the message. If you prefer, you can squirt water from a plastic spray bottle. Don't smack your pet; cats bruise easily and, in any case, smacking is not very effective. The cat will associate smacking with you, which may make it wary of you, while the magazine or the water seems to arrive out of the blue, as a consequence of what it is doing. Also, trying to smack a cat often results in a chase and the cat may get the idea that a delightful scratch will be followed by a jolly game. Once you have scared the cat off the wrong place, take it to the scratching post and encourage it to use it.

You can protect particular trouble spots, like the arms of your favourite chair, with strong plastic, so that it is not ruined while you work on the discipline. Cats dislike the feel of plastic so your pet will no longer scratch there – but, of course, it may well find a substitute spot. If your cat is really wily, it may find a quiet spot behind the settee to scratch in peace, where newspapers and squirted water cannot reach and then you may have to rely on aversion therapy.

Balloons can be very effective in this situation. Begin by sitting yourself on the floor and blowing up a couple of balloons. By now your cat will have come to join you and as it gives an investigative sniff, burst a balloon in its face. If it comes back, burst a second balloon; if it only watches from a wary distance, let the balloon go, so that it zooms across the room as it deflates. By now your cat should have decided that it will steer clear of balloons in future, so a couple of inflated balloons behind the settee will keep it away – though you may have to reinforce the treatment from time to time. You should find that balloons hung from the branches of your Christmas tree will discourage a cat that persistently attacks the decorations.

Soiling

If a previously 'clean' cat starts urinating or defecating in the wrong place, there may be a good reason for it. It may be that you have changed the position of the litter tray or the type of the litter, that it is too near the cat's food or you are not cleaning the tray often enough for your fastidious pet. If you have two cats sharing a tray, try giving them a tray each. Your cat may dislike the smell of the disinfectant you are using and if this is the case, you can get rid of it by putting a little baking soda in the final rinse. Soiling can be a sign of stress or anger, so if your cat is upset from a recent journey or a stay at a cattery, the behaviour will probably be temporary. If none of these reasons applies, or the cat shows any signs of being off colour, you should ask your vet to give it a checkup.

As with a kitten, you will need to be watchful and stop the behaviour every time (see page 33). Never use the old method of rubbing your cat's nose in the mess; it will probably like the smell and come back for more. Use the rolled-up newspaper and the firm 'No' whenever you see something unpleasant about to happen. If you are out for part of the day, or the soiling has already become a habit, confine your cat to the room where the litter tray is situated, except for the times when you can keep a sharp eye on its behaviour. If messes keep occurring when you are not there to prevent it, keep a bottle of white vinegar handy. Take the cat over to its dirt, so that it can smell it, then make sure it gets a good whiff of the vinegar. Use the vinegar as part of the cleaning up process so that if the cat returns to the spot, it will smell vinegar (which most cats loathe) rather than its own reassuring smell.

Spraying

Even neutered cats sometimes begin spraying walls or furniture inside the house and, though their urine does not have the pungent tom-cat smell, it will not add to the ambience of your home. This behaviour usually begins because of a change within the household or some form of extra stress that has upset the cat. It may be as simple as a new carpet or it may be a response to a cat that has just moved in next door, threatening your cat's territory. A new baby, death or divorce in the family, or moving house, may trigger spraying and some cats react to their owners' stress in this way.

If possible, refrain from scolding your cat as this will only add to the stress and can make its behaviour worse. The more secure and certain your cat feels of its place in the family, the more quickly it will get over this phase. If you have several cats and one or more is spraying you may be able to improve the situation by feeding them separately, or at least separating their feeding bowls as far as possible. A cat needs its own territory so each one should have its own special sleeping place.

Aggressive behaviour

Scratching and biting is behaviour that should be stopped the moment it starts. 'No', followed by a short period of ignoring the cat, will probably be sufficient. So long as you are consistent your cat will soon learn that a pleasurable game quickly comes to an end if claws or teeth come into play. Never make the mistake of snatching your hand away from a scratch, as the cat's natural reaction is to grab harder and the scratch will be far worse. If a cat bites, don't pull away but push your hand further into its mouth and it will quickly release you.

Many owners find that their cats roll over, apparently presenting their tummies to be tickled, then close on the petting hand like a vice, biting and scratching. This is not spite: it happens because humans misunderstand the feline signals. Though it may look as though you are expected to pet the exposed tummy, some cats will never allow this and if they do, it is the sign of a very close relationship. Cats often fight when lying on their backs, so that they can employ all their claws and teeth, and your fingers moving on this sensitive area seem to spark the defensive instinct and the cat automatically attacks.

If your normally gentle and affectionate cat suddenly becomes aggressive when touched, it is worthwhile checking with the vet as it may be suffering from an unsuspected illness.

Some cats are quiet and docile at home but very aggressive towards other cats. Though this is less likely after neutering, some neuters remain very territorial and will persecute any local cat that dares to step out of its house. You may be able to break up a cat fight with a broom, holding off one of the contenders with the bristles; otherwise you will need a bucket of water. If you need to pick up a furious or panic-stricken cat garden gloves are a wise precaution but even better is a blanket, which you can throw over the cat before you scoop it up.

6

Breeding

Like any serious hobby, that of cat breeding should not be entered into lightly or for the wrong reasons. You must desire to breed cats for personal satisfaction rather than financial gain, and you must have sufficient funds available to feed and house the cats adequately and safely, and be prepared to gain enough knowledge to care for your felines in sickness as well as in health, as newborn babies and as geriatrics. Breeding pedigree cats is a hobby full of rewards, even though these will never be financial. There is a great sense of pride and achievement in planning a litter and then rearing it, and great happiness may be derived from caring for the brood queen and her kittens from birth through weaning. Later, when your kittens grow and develop into prize winners on the show bench, your pride may know no bounds, and you will feel well on the way to the establishment of your own distinctive bloodlines in your chosen breed.

While it seems logical to the novice to buy a breeding pair of cats, this is impractical; a male is not content with one queen, and is a nuisance as a pet due to his adult habit of spray-marking his territory. Keeping a stud male is a job for the experienced fancier. So, once you have chosen the breed in which you want to specialize, buy one or two of the very best females that you can afford. Two kittens will keep each other company and will provide healthy competition for one another during their formative months of growth. It is quite a good idea to buy unrelated female kittens if you can, so that in later years, having kept further stock, you can mate together unrelated offspring with your own cattery name. You will find suitable cats at stud, with experienced owners full of useful advice, when your females are ready for mating.

The queen

A kitten for eventual breeding should be purchased at about three months old, though if you have the chance to buy an older kitten that has already proved its potential in the show ring so much the better. It is not necessary for her to have taken the top honours so long as she is sound and has an impeccable pedigree. She should be properly registered with a bona fide body that registers cats and runs cat shows, and have had a suitable course of vaccinations. She should be well grown, healthy and free from parasites, and come from a cattery or home where a programme of testing for freedom from feline infectious leukaemia is carried out.

A novice breeder should join a breed group and attend as many seminars and teach-ins as possible while the kitten is young. Cat shows are held around the country and at such events the novice can meet and talk with other fanciers of his or her chosen breed.

From the age of three months the female kitten may be allowed to live a fairly normal life within the family, though she should usually be kept safely indoors away from health hazards and traffic. The little female should be fed a sensible, well-balanced diet, and encouraged to play in order to keep fit. Daily grooming will help to keep her coat in good condition and her muscles toned, and such sessions also help to strengthen the bond between cat and owner.

Though the kitten's first period of heat or oestrus may occur at any time from four months onwards, most young queens of Siamese or Oriental breeds start to 'call' at about nine months old, while the Persians and Shorthairs may not 'call' until well over one year old.

It is best to merely observe the young cat the first time she comes on heat, and to make sure that she is safely confined indoors or in a secure pen until the oestrus has passed. By noting her symptoms and behaviour you will be able to monitor subsequent periods of oestrus. At her next 'call' you may wish to have her mated, and if so you must make arrangements with the owner of a suitable stud cat, found by visiting cat shows or by reading advertisements in the cat press.

Some cats mature early and may 'call' at three- or four-week intervals from a very young age. In this case your veterinary surgeon may advise early mating rather than risk a setback in your kitten's health, for frequent 'calling' can cause loss of appetite and, therefore, loss of condition at a critical period in the cat's development. Continued periods of heat without conception can also lead to sterility in later life. Your veterinary surgeon will check your kitten to make sure that she is physically fit for motherhood. Pregnancy often completes the growth and maturity of well-grown youngsters if they are well fed and correctly cared for during this important stage.

The stud male

Though the brood queen plays a vital part in the breeding programme, the stud male's role is perhaps even more important, for he may be responsible for hundreds of kittens during his working life, while even the most fertile queen is only likely to produce a maximum of one hundred. For this reason the stud male must be an excellent example of his breed, selected for his good looks, which should approximate closely to the breed standard of points of excellence, for his general health and stature, and for his gentle temperament. He should have been well reared and from a strong litter that suffered no setbacks during the kittens' early days. The qualities and fertility records of both his parents should be known.

Keeping a stud male properly requires experience and understanding. Such cats are generally loving and affectionate, but their habit of spray-marking their territory and possessions means that they usually have to be housed well away from the family's rooms. It is important, however, for the stud cat to be kept occupied and interested in life during the periods between visiting queens. He will need lots of affection and daily handling, even short-coated cats benefiting from daily grooming. His accommodation should be as pleasant and spacious as possible, with plenty of exercise areas and access to suitable spots for sunning and running.

Each owner has his or her own ideas about the ideal construction of stud accommodation, but its siting is very important and should be adjacent to areas of general daily activity. Kennels, stables, summerhouses and workshops have all been successfully converted into stud homes. The basic requirements are a building tall enough to allow you to stand inside and with a large enough floor area to enable you to comfortably attend to the daily needs of the male and his visiting females, and to adequately supervise matings. It should be large enough also for the male cat to take exercise during long winter months when he may not wish to use his outdoor run. All interior walls should be lined and insulated, and all the surfaces should be completely washable. The floor, in particular, will receive very hard wear and be subjected to urine spray. The walls may be lined with laminated boards or may be sealed and painted with washable paint. The floor may be tiled or fitted with impervious, vinyl-coated material, and all cracks and crevices should be adequately sealed.

A pen or cage must be provided for the visiting queens, and opinions vary as to the ideal size for this. Some catteries provide very large pens and runs, but the queen is at stud for a limited time, during which she is likely to be very preoccupied with the important matter in hand. It seems more logical, therefore, to make most of the stud-house space available to the male cat, who is in occupation at all times. The queen's pen should be draughtproof and cosy, with one side of wire mesh so that the two cats can get to know one another. It must be large enough to hold the visiting queen's bed and toilet tray, and have room for her to exercise and for her food and water bowls. It is perhaps best sited well above the floor, unless it is of walk-in height, for the stud male may try to spray the queen's bedding and belongings if these are at floor level.

The stud house should be enclosed in a pleasant, safely wired run. The floor should be paved or concreted, for grass soon becomes soiled and is impossible to sterilize. It is a good idea to have part of the run covered to give exercise space in inclement weather, and the door to the stud house should be angled to avoid prevailing winds. Logs and shelves provide climbing and sunning facilities. The entrance gates must be well constructed and fasten securely.

A cat chosen as a potential stud will be shown to championship status (see page 121) in order to prove his quality and may even go on to become a grand or supreme champion. He will be carefully reared through kittenhood, and be fed to grow strong and healthy. His vaccination programmes will be meticulously carried out and regular booster injections given. He will be regularly dosed against internal parasites and his teeth, ears and claws will be examined weekly. His owner will arrange for regular swabs to be taken to check his freedom from any viral infections brought in by visiting queens, and for regular blood testing for feline leukaemia virus.

When a stud cat loses his popularity, the caring owner will have him neutered rather than let him become more and more morose living in a state of frustrated boredom. Though many neutered ex-studs continue to spray, and are, therefore, unable to become house pets, their busy youth should have entitled them to a long and peaceful retirement. Ex-stud cats, which would have fought each other to the death during their working lives, often settle down to live out their days together.

Supervised matings

The first queens mated by a young stud should be steady and experienced. Feline mating procedures often seem quite terrifying to the casual observer as the mated queen quickly and sometimes viciously attacks the male, who must be quick enough to jump sharply out of reach of her flashing claws. A quieter, older queen may growl and hiss, but her swiping paws will be merely feints and not intended to hurt. It is important that the male's first sexual encounters are well supervised to guard against him being injured or frustrated.

When the visiting queen is delivered by her owner, she should be put quietly and gently into the special queen's pen in the stud house. Her owner may be allowed to put the queen into the pen and to settle her down. If this is permitted, the stud cat should be shut out in his run while the human visitor invades his territory for he may decide to mark the visitor in the friendliest way he knows – with a well-directed spray of urine.

Once the queen is settled, the stud cat will show great interest in her. Though she is likely to spit, snarl and growl at his advances, he is well protected from her teeth and claws by the wiremesh partition. The stud should have been given a really good meal before the queen's arrival, for he may refuse all food from the time she is in residence until he has successfully mated with her. The cats must be kept apart until the queen shows signs of being ready for mating. This can take up to thirty-six hours with the maiden queen, and less than one hour with a more experienced one. The signs of readiness include vigorous rolling and stretching, the queen's growls and hisses stopping or becoming rather half-hearted, and she may make welcoming cries in answer to the stud male's encouraging crooning.

Before the queen is released a coarse woven rug should be placed on the floor and the stud house door closed. Most stud owners keep a special mating rug for their cats. It is taken away when not in use so that it does not become impregnated with spray, and brought in specially for mating times. The stud soon recognizes the appearance of his rug and fully realizes its implication. Closing the door cuts down the area in which the queen may run around, pretending to avoid the stud cat's advances, while the rug gives her a warm place on which to roll and provides her with a surface to grip for stability during mating. The stud's owner should sit quietly and not interfere with the mating, which may take some time while the stud manoeuvres the queen into position. After mating, the male cat will leap away from the queen on to his shelf or stool, and the queen should be allowed to settle down. Then she should be replaced in her pen to rest before a repeat mating is allowed.

The brood queen

A queen can breed quite satisfactorily for a number of years provided that she is kept fit and well fed and not allowed to produce and rear too many kittens each year. A queen that starts breeding at about ten months old and then has one or two litters each year will probably breed successfully until the age of eight or nine. Lactating to feed a litter of five or more kittens takes much more out of a queen than the process of pregnancy and birth, and too frequent or too lengthy periods of lactation can seriously deplete the mother's calcium reserves. A breeder must be watchful, and ensure that an adequate level of calcium is present in an easily assimilable form in the queen's diet and, if in any doubt, should seek veterinary advice.

The cat does not have a specific breeding season, and may be in breeding condition for most of the year, with peaks in early spring, early summer and occasionally at the onset of autumn. Cats kept indoors with longer than natural periods of white light tend to breed more frequently than those kept in a cattery with normal hours of daylight and darkness. Kittens born in the spring are generally easier to rear and often appear more robust than those born at other times, and spring and summer kittens are able to spend time in the sunshine, which is of definite benefit to them.

During oestrus the queen must be carefully confined. If she is to be mated to a pedigree stud, she will be taken for service on the second or third day, but may try to get out of the house before this. Queens have been known to jump from very high windows and escape through very narrow apertures to gain their freedom while on heat, so extra vigilance is essential. Even if the calling queen does not mate with a stray tom, she may well pick up an infection or parasites, or could be killed or injured on the road. Some female cats call at regular, well-spaced intervals, while others seem to be perpetually in some stage of heat unless pregnant or lactating. Cats of Foreign and Oriental breeds seem to call more than Persians or Shorthairs.

A rather strange phenomenon that occurs in some cats is the urge to mate again after three or four weeks, even though safely and sometimes obviously pregnant. Cats kept in small breeding colonies for research and study have been observed to do this, and some breeders have been caught out by it. Seeing a queen rolling and calling again, the obvious response is to assume that the first mating was unsuccessful and arrange for the queen to go back to the stud male and mate again. The breeder will then be taken completely by surprise when the queen produces normal kittens some sixty-five days after the first mating! No one is quite sure why some queens act in this way, but one theory suggests that the act of mating again stimulates certain hormone production, and may help with the processes of birth and subsequent lactation.

Occasionally a queen will appear to come into heat almost immediately after giving birth, rolling and calling in a manner typical of oestrus. She is unlikely to mate, however, and the scent of her lactation appears to repel other cats, including entire males, which tend to spit at her and keep their distance. Even when a queen nursing young kittens does mate, she rarely conceives, possibly because her hormone balance prevents implantation of the fertilized ova.

Going to stud

The young queen must be treated kindly and tenderly during her first period of oestrus. She will be under considerable stress and may react uncharacteristically. She may be unusually affectionate, and also hypersensitive to being touched – purring and rubbing one moment, spitting and biting the next. She should be kept as calm and quiet as possible, and should not be subjected to any unnecessary strain. It is unwise to mate the young queen, for she should be allowed to use this period to become accustomed to the new sensations within her body without the added stress of travel and confinement with a strange male cat in an unknown environment.

The breeder should make the necessary arrangements with the stud owner for the queen to mate on her second heat. It is usual to telephone on the first day of the queen's oestrus, arranging to transport her on the second or third day. The queen should be rolling as well as calling before she is taken to stud. The journey may upset her sufficiently to stop the calling, but once she is actually rolling it is unlikely that any minor upset will interfere with the natural breeding process. During her trips to and from stud, the queen should be transported in a wicker, wood or plastic-covered mesh carrier, which must fasten securely and be escape-proof.

It is usually necessary to leave the queen at stud for three or four days. The first day is spent becoming acclimatized to both the stud quarters and the close proximity of the male cat, separated from her by a wire-mesh grille. The queen is generally ready to mate by the following day, and the two cats are allowed together. Mating may be repeated two or three times before the cats are separated, and the process is repeated again the following day. Some stud owners allow the two cats to live together once the first successful mating has been observed and the animals have shown themselves to be totally compatible. They will mate many times during their time together, and will curl up in the same box to sleep. As the act of mating stimulates the release of the queen's ova, repeated matings generally ensure that the queen is safely in kitten before she returns home. When collected by the breeder, the queen will still be well in heat and must be safely confined indoors or in a pen until the oestrus diminishes. During the period she should be kept as quiet as possible and fed her normal nourishing meals.

Gestation Table

This table allows a ready reference for calculating the date on which kittens are due to be born. To use the table, first look up the date on which the queen was mated, then read off the date below. For example: a cat mated on April 1 will be due to have kittens on June 5.

January

1	2	3	4	5	6	7	8	9	10	11	12	13	14	15	16
7	8	9	10	11	12	13	14	15	16	17	18	19	20	21	22

MARCH

17	18	19	20	21	22	23	24	25	26	27	28	29	30	31
23	24	25	26	27	28	29	30	31	1	2	3	4	5	6

MARCH   *APRIL*

February

1	2	3	4	5	6	7	8	9	10	11	12	13	14	15	16
7	8	9	10	11	12	13	14	15	16	17	18	19	20	21	22

APRIL

17	18	19	20	21	22	23	24	25	26	27	28
23	24	25	26	27	28	29	30	1	2	3	4

APRIL   *MAY*

March

1	2	3	4	5	6	7	8	9	10	11	12	13	14	15	16
5	6	7	8	9	10	11	12	13	14	15	16	17	18	19	20

MAY

17	18	19	20	21	22	23	24	25	26	27	28	29	30	31
21	22	23	24	25	26	27	28	29	30	31	1	2	3	4

MAY   *JUNE*

April

1	2	3	4	5	6	7	8	9	10	11	12	13	14	15	16
5	6	7	8	9	10	11	12	13	14	15	16	17	18	19	20

JUNE

17	18	19	20	21	22	23	24	25	26	27	28	29	30
21	22	23	24	25	26	27	28	29	30	1	2	3	4

JUNE   *JULY*

May

1	2	3	4	5	6	7	8	9	10	11	12	13	14	15	16
5	6	7	8	9	10	11	12	13	14	15	16	17	18	19	20

JULY

17	18	19	20	21	22	23	24	25	26	27	28	29	30	31
21	22	23	24	25	26	27	28	29	30	31	1	2	3	4

JULY   *AUGUST*

June

1	2	3	4	5	6	7	8	9	10	11	12	13	14	15	16
5	6	7	8	9	10	11	12	13	14	15	16	17	18	19	20

AUGUST

17	18	19	20	21	22	23	24	25	26	27	28	29	30
21	22	23	24	25	26	27	28	29	30	31	1	2	3

AUGUST   *SEPTEMBER*

July

1	2	3	4	5	6	7	8	9	10	11	12	13	14	15	16
4	5	6	7	8	9	10	11	12	13	14	15	16	17	18	19

SEPTEMBER

17	18	19	20	21	22	23	24	25	26	27	28	29	30	31
20	21	22	23	24	25	26	27	28	29	30	1	2	3	4

SEPTEMBER   *OCTOBER*

August	1	2	3	4	5	6	7	8	9	10	11	12	13	14	15	16
	5	6	7	8	9	10	11	12	13	14	15	16	17	18	19	20

OCTOBER

	17	18	19	20	21	22	23	24	25	26	27	28	29	30	31
	21	22	23	24	25	26	27	28	29	30	31	1	2	3	4

OCTOBER   *NOVEMBER*

September	1	2	3	4	5	6	7	8	9	10	11	12	13	14	15	16
	5	6	7	8	9	10	11	12	13	14	15	16	17	18	19	20

NOVEMBER

	17	18	19	20	21	22	23	24	25	26	27	28	29	30	31
	21	22	23	24	25	26	27	28	29	30	31	1	2	3	4

NOVEMBER   *DECEMBER*

October	1	2	3	4	5	6	7	8	9	10	11	12	13	14	15	16
	5	6	7	8	9	10	11	12	13	14	15	16	17	18	19	20

DECEMBER

	17	18	19	20	21	22	23	24	25	26	27	28	29	30	31
	21	22	23	24	25	26	27	28	29	30	31	1	2	3	4

DECEMBER   *JANUARY*

November	1	2	3	4	5	6	7	8	9	10	11	12	13	14	15	16
	5	6	7	8	9	10	11	12	13	14	15	16	17	18	19	20

JANUARY

	17	18	19	20	21	22	23	24	25	26	27	28	29	30	31
	21	22	23	24	25	26	27	28	29	30	31	1	2	3	4

JANUARY   *FEBRUARY*

December	1	2	3	4	5	6	7	8	9	10	11	12	13	14	15	16
	4	5	6	7	8	9	10	11	12	13	14	15	16	17	18	19

FEBRUARY

	17	18	19	20	21	22	23	24	25	26	27	28	29	30	31
	20	21	22	23	24	25	26	27	28	1	2	3	4	5	6

FEBRUARY   *MARCH*

The pregnant queen

It may be difficult to tell whether or nor a queen is safely in kitten, but careful inspection of the nipples each day will reveal the condition known as 'pinking-up' – the nipples look slightly enlarged and very pink on about the twenty-first day after conception, having looked normal the previous day – and this is a very hopeful sign that a cat is pregnant. Gestation in the cat seems to average sixty-five days, though kittens may survive if born fifty-nine to seventy days after mating. Throughout the gestation period the queen should be treated quite normally and should not be fussed, for over-humanized queens usually make dreadful mothers. The spoiled queen may refuse to look after her kittens unless her owner stays beside her and lends a hand; she may be constantly stressed and so produce acid milk, which adversely affects the litter; and she may constantly carry the kittens in and out of the nest box, becoming more and more distressed and perhaps lacerating their necks in the process. The normal, well-balanced and properly treated queen will sail through her period of pregnancy, birth and motherhood without encountering any serious problems, and will, in turn, rear normal, healthy, well-balanced kittens.

Pregnancy guide

Weeks One to Three
Appearance Normal, no increase in girth apparent. Nipples may look pink and enlarged on twenty-first day.
Behaviour Normal, except that some morning sickness may be noticed on queen's return from stud.
Treatment Normal, except that the diet may be changed slightly, giving easily digested, nourishing meals on her return from stud. If the queen runs a temperature, seems listless or is off her food, veterinary advice should be sought.

Week Four
Appearance Abdomen appears slightly swollen. A veterinary surgeon may be able to feel the tiny embryonic kittens by palpation, but this must *not* be attempted by the inexperienced, as careless probing can cause the queen internal damage.
Behaviour Calm and very relaxed. The queen may seek out and chew special grasses if allowed her freedom to roam in the garden.
Treatment Normal; careful grooming helps to keep the coat and skin in good condition and the muscles toned.

Week Five

Appearance Abdomen is visibly swollen in action and repose, and nipples are definitely enlarged.

Behaviour Very calm and relaxed.

Treatment Normal; careful grooming continues and an extra high-protein meal should be added each day.

Week Six

Appearance Queen looks obviously pregnant, even to the casual observer.

Behaviour Seems less inclined to exercise and takes extra care when jumping up or down; appetite increases.

Treatment Extra calcium may be given; some cats can assimilate milk, and evaporated milk is easier to digest than fresh cow's milk. Encourage the queen to take exercise through play – for example, get her to chase a feather tied to string – but do not allow her to become overtired or to jump and twist her body too vigorously.

Week Seven

Appearance The kittens may be seen moving in the queen's abdomen.

Behaviour Seems to enjoy the process of 'quickening' and rolls and stretches herself sinuously along the floor. The quickening also appears to trigger off the nesting instinct, and the queen may start to search out a suitable place for giving birth.

Treatment Careful feeding of three good meals a day, continuing to ensure that adequate minerals and vitamins are provided. Daily grooming to tone the body and to remove dead hairs and flakes of skin should continue. A large cardboard box should be provided, with a hole cut in the side for the queen's access, and a pile of newspapers and pieces of kitchen paper placed inside for her to tear up to form a soft bed. Special heated pads can be purchased, which are perfectly safe and can be placed under the bedding, giving a low, gentle heat, ideal for kittening and during the first few weeks of rearing the litter.

Some breeders use special kittening boxes of wood or plastics, but the humble cardboard box is cheap and ideal, for it may be discarded when soiled and replaced by another, eliminating the risk of any build-up of infection.

Weeks Eight and Nine

Appearance The queen's abdomen becomes hard and rather pear-shaped. Her breasts are noticeably enlarged. Her coat should be in very good condition, but with small flakes of dandruff apparent in darker-coated breeds.

Behaviour The queen spends extra time in self-grooming, paying particular attention to her breasts. She is extra-affectionate, and goes to her box from time to time, tearing the paper into shreds with her teeth and claws as her time draws nearer. A few days prior to kittening, the queen's voice changes dramatically, and this is particularly noticeable in the vocal Foreign and Oriental breeds. Just before birth, the queen will refuse her food and become restless; she may get up and flop down several times as if trying to find a comfortable position. When the birth is imminent, she may go repeatedly to her toilet tray.

Treatment The queen should be lovingly cared for, groomed daily, and fed on four small, very nourishing meals of her favourite foods, with suitable vitamin and mineral supplements. As she may be too bulky to attend properly to her anal area, this region should be gently cleansed every day with soft tissues, soft soap and warm water, then dried carefully, and talcum powder may be applied. The nipples should be checked, and if dry or cracked they should be gently massaged with vegetable oil. In the Longhair queen, the hair should be gently clipped away from around the nipples and the genital area, using blunt-ended scissors. Check the queen's coat for parasites by using a very fine-toothed metal comb (never use pest powder on pregnant cats). Ensure the ears are clean and her teeth are in a healthy condition. It is often advisable to have the queen checked by the veterinary surgeon to make sure all is well prior to the birth.

The Birth

The kittening kit
Small squares of terry towelling, boiled to sterilize, and then air dried and stored in a polythene bag.
A bottle of astringent antiseptic, obtained from the veterinary surgeon, to seal the kittens' umbilical cords.
A pair of blunt-tipped scissors, sterilized by boiling and stored in a polythene bag.
Cottonwool.
Roll of absorbent paper towelling.
Hot-water bottle or electric heating pad, wrapped in clean linen towel.
Bag or bin for soiled equipment.

First-stage labour
When the queen's labour starts her rectal temperature drops from its normal 38–38.6°C (100.4–101.5°F) to 36.6–37.2°C (98–99°F). She may pace the floor, wail continuously, groan, growl, go in and out of her kittening box, tear paper, go in and out of her litter tray and vomit. Instead, however, she may just sit quietly, purring and kneading with her forepaws.

Slight uterine contractions may be noticed as ripples along her flanks when the first kitten moves from the uterine horn to the uterus, and these contractions may be accompanied by a break in the rhythm of the queen's breathing or purring. The queen may pant, growl or tremble with the contractions. This stage can last up to twenty-four hours.

Second-stage labour
Most queens go into their nesting box as second-stage labour commences. Some want to be with their owners during this stage, while others are happier left alone in the dark, and in this case the breeder should look into the box from time to time to check that everything is going well.

Fierce contractions are seen as the first kitten moves into the birth canal. Contractions may occur every half-hour at first, increasing to every thirty seconds just prior to the birth. Kittens may be born in rapid succession, or at lengthy intervals; the queen usually deals with cleaning away the membrane, severing the cord and disposing of the placenta. When the last kitten is born she settles down to rest and to nurse the litter.

A normal birth

The kitten is normally delivered in its sac within twenty minutes, and immediately it is expelled it flexes its neck to free its head from the membranes and takes its first gulp of air. The mother licks the kitten quite roughly, drying its body, and eats the membranes. As the kitten's breathing reflex is stimulated, it squeaks and flexes its body. The placenta is attached to the kitten by the umbilical cord, and as the queen moves, or gives another contraction, the placenta passes out of her vagina. The queen normally eats the placenta and along the cord, stopping a couple of centimetres from the kitten's body.

An assisted birth

Human intervention in the kittening process is only necessary when things go wrong, or if the queen gives birth so quickly that she is unable to cope with each kitten in turn. Too many breeders fuss and interfere, pulling each kitten into the world, cleaning it, tying and cutting the cord, and disposing of each placenta. This is quite inexcusable, for it has been proved that naturally delivered animals fare far better than those assisted into the world. The breeder should be on hand, prepared and ready to help in an emergency.

If a kitten remains in a half-presented position for some time, despite constant straining by the queen, you are justified in lending a hand. The kitten born safe inside its sac usually slides easily through the birth passage like a well-lubricated capsule. If the sac has ruptured and the fluid expelled, the kitten begins to dry out and it may become stuck. Put a square of terry towelling over the exposed portion of the kitten, and wait until the queen contracts. Then, gently ease the small body out and down, in a curved movement between the queen's hindlegs towards her belly. Do not pull hard, and make certain that you get the angle correct so as not to hurt the queen, timing the tension to coincide with her straining. The queen may growl or cry out, and will then rest once the kitten is freed. Do not pull on the umbilical cord until the next contraction, and hold it with a piece of terry towelling rather than in the fingers. Be careful not to pull on the umbilicus, or the kitten may develop a hernia at the navel.

Put the kitten near the queen's head so that she can clean it, but if she refuses, clean its face, nostrils and mouth with some kitchen paper. The kitten should breathe before the cord is broken or cut. With luck, the placenta will pass easily, and the queen should be encouraged to eat it. If you need to dry and clean the kitten, use kitchen paper to mop up the amniotic fluid and to wipe away the membranes from its body, and then rub it dry with a square of terry towelling. If its breathing sounds bubbly, hold the kitten firmly in the hand and swing it head down in a smooth arc from waist height to your knee two or three times to clear the mucus from its lungs and nasal passages. Then, with its head still lower than its body, hold it on one hand while you rub the body from tail down to head with the towelling square.

There is no urgency about severing the umbilical cord and, in fact, it is best to wait as long as possible in case the cat decides to take over once more. If you do have to deal with the cord, use the sterilized scissors to cut it a couple of centimetres from the kitten's body. There is no need to tie the cord first, just dip a piece of cottonwool into the astringent antiseptic lotion and use this to hold the cord between the thumb and forefinger of one hand, near the kitten's body. Cut the cord close to your fingers and press the cottonwool over the cut end, squeezing tightly for a moment or two while the end seals to ensure that bacteria cannot enter the stump. Within a few days the cord will dry and fall away leaving a neat navel.

If the queen needs assistance with all the kittens, deal with each one in the same way, putting one kitten on a wrapped hot-water bottle or heated pad while you deal with the next. The chances are that after the last kitten is born the queen will contentedly gather them to her to nurse.

If you cannot deliver a kitten, or the queen strains to no avail and no portion of the kitten can be seen, you should call your vet for assistance. It is normally advisable to take the queen, in her maternity box if possible, to the vet, in case surgery is required. Try to get someone else to drive so that you are free to comfort your cat during the journey.

Sometimes, matters may be righted by a hormone injection to encourage contractions, while in others, the vet needs to manipulate a tiny limb into a better position to allow natural birth. The best presentation for a kitten is the 'diving' position, where it comes head first with its forepaws tucked up under the chin. The tail-first presentation causes few difficulties either, as the kitten's tail and extended hindlegs are presented first and the rest of the body follows quite easily. The butt presentation is fairly easy to deal with, the tail and rump coming first with the hindlegs pointing towards the kitten's head. Problems mainly occur when the kitten is turned so that the back of its neck is presented first and the shoulders cause a blockage, and manipulation can often rectify the kitten's position. However, when the queen's pelvis is small and the kitten large, any but the best presentation can prove impossible.

Caesarean section

When there is no alternative, the veterinary surgeon will deliver the kittens by opening the queen's abdomen. This operation is known as a Caesarean section and is carried out under general anaesthetic. Unless affected by the anaesthetic, the kittens are usually quite strong and may be passed to the breeder waiting in the anteroom to be dried and stimulated, while the queen is stitched up and brought round. The queen may be allowed home, but if she has reacted badly to the operation she will be kept in the veterinary hospital under observation, and the breeder may be asked to take the kittens home without the mother. The kittens need not be fed for several hours, by which time the queen may be ready to accept them.

Some queens resent kittens born by such unnatural means, and need great encouragement before they will nurse their litter. The hormone balance is very disturbed at this time, so patience is needed. As soon as the milk supply starts, the queen's natural instincts should prevail, but it may be necessary to hold the queen firmly while the kittens are encouraged to suck, after which she should be petted and fussed. Within a week matters are usually normal, but in rare cases it is necessary to treat the kittens as orphans, fostering them with another queen or hand-rearing them. The queen's stitches are removed after seven to ten days.

Hand-rearing kittens

While the best way of rearing orphan or rejected kittens is to find a foster mother, this is not always easy. A foster queen needs to have had her litter as near to the kittens' birth as possible so that the milk will be at the right strength. Sometimes veterinary surgeons can help, having been asked for euthanasia for an unwanted litter. The newborn kittens are first rubbed all over with the foster mother's bedding and then are placed between her hindlegs to crawl forward towards her stomach. It can take some time before the foster mother will accept the youngsters, and the breeder needs great patience. The kittens should not be left alone at this time in case they are rejected and injured, but once they have nursed and the queen has cleaned them, they will be all right and can safely be left.

If no foster mother is available, the litter may be hand-reared, but this is not a task to be undertaken lightly. The kittens must be kept at a constant temperature of 27–30°C (81–86°F) for the first two weeks, gradually reducing to 21°C (70°F) by the age of six weeks, when they are well furred, and moving around and playing during waking hours. The best bedding is torn kitchen tissue, which is absorbent and comfortably warm if laid in a thick layer. The pieces should be torn so that they are not likely to entangle the kittens' legs, and any soiled pieces removed at each feeding time.

The breeder must mimic the mother's cleaning technique by using a piece of cottonwool or tissue, moistened with warm water, to clean the genital regions of the kittens after each feed. The queen would lick this area to stimulate urination and defecation, and it is important to ensure that each kitten empties itself. At birth, the kitten's bowel is filled with a dark sticky substance called meconium, and this can cause problems unless passed within the following three or four days. Such stools will be almost black in colour, and the breeder should note which kittens have passed them. Normal stools are yellow-orange in colour. After washing the kittens, dry them carefully and use a little talcum powder if necessary to keep them dry and fresh. Any soreness can be treated with a light smear of petroleum jelly.

Feeding

Feeding the kittens is done at two-hourly intervals day and night for the first week. It is possible to leave a four-hour break from midnight to 4a.m. during the second week, extending this from midnight to 6a.m. during the third week unless the kittens' digestions seem to be suffering, or they wake and are fretful. All the other milk feeds should be given every two hours without fail, even if the kittens have to be wakened for them. This is obviously a demanding time, requiring patience and fortitude. Luckily, from three to four weeks of age the kittens will show an interest in solid food, and gradually the milk feeds can be spread apart. By six weeks, they will be having five small meals daily and the breeder is able to catch up on his lost sleep.

The most important aspect of bottle feeding is the maintenance of strict hygiene. Kittens feeding from their mother obtain antibodies in her milk to fight off infection, but bottle-reared youngsters do not. All their feeding equipment must be properly cleaned and sterilized every time it is used. The milk feeds should always be freshly made and be at the correct temperature. Kittens may be bottle fed with a syringe or dropper, with a short piece of rubber tube over the tip to encourage the kitten to suck, but by far the best utensil is a proper kitten-feeding bottle, complete with correctly shaped teats.

The feeds can be made up using specially formulated powdered milk, which simulates the queen's milk, or, in an emergency, evaporated cow's milk may be used diluted with an equal quantity of boiled water. During the first week, 3 to 5 millilitres ($\frac{1}{2}$–1 teaspoon) are sufficient for each kitten at each feed, increasing to about 7 millilitres ($1\frac{1}{2}$ teaspoons) at two weeks of age and 10 millilitres (2 teaspoons) at three weeks. The kittens must be allowed to suck at their own speed and not hurried in any way. While feeding they should be encouraged to knead with their forepaws, and this can be done by allowing the kitten to feed with its stomach and chest across the bare forearm, giving warmth and comfort, as well as supplying a suitable surface for the tiny kneading paws. At first the sucking reflex may be difficult to stimulate, and the teat should be put into the kitten's mouth and gently lifted upwards before starting to withdraw it again. If a drop of milk is expressed before this is done, the kitten should soon start to suck.

Rearing kittens

The normal litter will settle down immediately after birth, and the queen, having cleaned the kittens and her own flanks and legs, will rest. She should be given a nourishing drink at this time, and most acceptable is a concoction made from one beaten egg, one teaspoon of glucose and two tablespoons of boiling water. Most queens will gulp this down with relish before settling down with the litter, and will then be happy to rest undisturbed for several hours. When she stirs, the queen should be encouraged to stretch her legs and to use her litter tray, but she may be reluctant to leave her kittens.

Many breeders change the nest material at this stage, and the easiest way is to use a firm pad of paper or blanket covered with a smooth pillowcase or sheet, all folded to the size of the base of the box. The kittens can be lifted quickly on to the fresh bedding, the soiled bedding removed from the box, and the kittens and new pad placed back in the nest. As kittens 'home in' on the scent of the birth excretions, it is advisable to put a little of the pink-stained papers back on top of the clean bedding, and this also helps the queen to relax. She may become distressed at having the bedding changed, and it is vitally important to keep her as calm and relaxed as possible during this stage. A fraught queen may decide to move the kittens, or she may lose her milk. The soiled paper bedding should be taken well away for disposal, as the queen may try to take her kittens to the bedding if she can scent the nesting material.

Regular checks

The queen must pass water within twenty-four hours of the birth. If she is reluctant to do this, lift her and place her in a clean litter tray at regular intervals until she gets the message and performs. Each kitten should be lifted and examined every day. The breeder must have clean, well-rinsed, carefully dried and warm hands, and a kitten should be lifted by enclosing its body in the hand, raising it gently and firmly, and holding it securely so that it feels safe. The body should feel firm and plump if the kitten is feeding well. Its face should be clean, there should be no stains under the tail, and the cord should have dried up and the navel area look normal. Danger signs include: noisy, squealing kittens which feel bony – these are not feeding well and may need supplementary meals until the queen's milk adjusts to the litter's needs; a raised, angry rim around the navel – this could mean that infection entered the severed cord and veterinary attention is required; yellow-orange staining down the kitten's hindlegs – this should be wiped away with warm water to encourage the queen to clean the region.

Most queens enjoy having the breeder examine and admire the kittens, but too many visitors, or inquisitive family pets, may upset her so much that she carries the kittens in and out of the box, possibly damaging them, so peace and quiet is essential. The queen rarely seems hungry after the birth if she has eaten the placentas and been given the nourishing milk, egg and glucose drink. Light feeds are best at this time – steamed fish, meat jelly and a little raw minced rabbit or other white meat, with a pinch of sterilized bonemeal for its calcium content.

For the first few days of life the kittens sleep and feed. Each kitten selects its own nipple and will prefer that feeding position from then on. Kittens may be seen to scrabble at one another's heads and shoulders, apparently fighting for a nipple, and this is quite normal behaviour. The queen's nipples must be examined on the day after the birth to ensure that milk is flowing properly and that there are no 'blind' breasts. Blocked breasts can be eased by gently bathing with hand-hot water and then massaging with warmed olive oil. If this treatment proves ineffective, veterinary advice is necessary to prevent milk fever or the formation of a breast abscess. A queen may have one or two permanently blind breasts, but as no milk is formed they cause little or no trouble and are usually superfluous, for the queen normally has eight breasts.

The queen can develop acid milk if her diet is unsuitable, or if she is continually stressed, worried or harassed. The litter may be lost if this condition is not recognized and treated in time. The first sign is that the kittens become increasingly restless and noisy. Veterinary treatment is required for the queen, and this combined with the feeding of a carefully chosen, bland diet should adjust the acid balance of the milk, resulting in contented kittens once more.

Weight
Kittens vary considerably in birth weight. Some Foreign and Oriental kittens may weigh as little as 57 grammes (2 ounces) at birth, while a Persian kitten can weigh double that. A small litter usually has bigger kittens than a large litter. Kittens born weighing less than 57 grammes (2 ounces) rarely survive to adulthood, even if they live through to weaning, and sickly kittens are often rejected by the queen, who may push them to the back of the nest and lie on them. Kittens increase in weight rapidly and should gain the equivalent of their individual birth weights each week, so a kitten weighing 85 grammes (3 ounces) at birth should weigh 255 grammes (9 ounces) at three weeks, provided the queen is adequately fed.

Sexing
Breeders are usually eager to determine the sex of newborn kittens, and it is quite easy for even the novice to tell males from females while the kittens are still damp, particularly if both sexes are present for comparison. In the female kitten the two tiny orifices – the round anus and the small, slit-shaped vagina – are close together, resembling an inverted exclamation mark. In the male, the tiny round anus is separated from the dot which

indicates the end of the penis by two small swellings, which are the testes. As the kittens grow it is sometimes possible to mistake their sex, but this can always be confirmed by the veterinary surgeon at vaccination time.

Development guide
The first 10 days. During this time, the kittens' eyes open. In some Foreign and Oriental breeds, the eyes may start to open on the second or third day, while in Shorthairs and Persians the eyes may stay tight shut for over a week. If the eyes water and the lids seal again, bathe them gently in warm water but do not attempt to open them manually. The kittens move around on their stomachs.

10–14 days. The kittens may hiss when picked up. Their legs become stronger.

14–21 days. The kittens look at one another and at the mother, start patting with their paws and rolling over.

21–28 days. They develop their walking skills until they walk with confidence, and begin to play.

4–6 weeks. At this stage, the kittens begin to show an interest in the queen's food but it is better to prepare a special mixture: some raw white meat or cooked and boned white fish reduced to a creamy consistency in a blender with a little water, with a pinch of bonemeal added, is ideal. Some owners feed baby cereal with tinned evaporated milk diluted with water but this may lead to diarrhoea in some breeds. The kittens begin learning to wash themselves. Some mothers look after the toilet training of the kittens; otherwise the owner can begin introducing kittens to the litter tray.

6–7 weeks. The owner should be providing small meals at regular intervals. Mix meat with a little gravy and canned cat food with a little boiled water – but not enough to make it mushy. Offer water at room temperature. The kittens will be practising hunting by now, chasing and ambushing one another.

8–10 weeks. The kittens should be fully weaned by now and eating well. They are independent enough to leave their mother.

7

Showing

The first cat show ever recorded was at St Giles Fair, Winchester in Hampshire, in 1598, though it bore no resemblance to the cat shows of today. The modern type of show, with cats exhibited in individual pens, began with a splendid affair organized by artist and writer Harrison Weir at London's Crystal Palace in 1871. Then in the year of Queen Victoria's Jubilee in 1887, when a four day show was held at Alexandra Palace, a group of cat fanciers joined forces to form the National Cat Club – and so the British Cat Fancy was born. Harrison Weir became the first elected president of the National Cat Club and for the next 23 years this body carried out the functions of registration, instituted championships and formulated rules and regulations governing the running of cat shows. The first official stud book was published in 1895.

A friendly rivalry was established when a strong band of Scottish fanciers got together and began staging shows in Glasgow. Several other clubs and societies were formed, all agreeing to run their shows under the rules of the National Cat Club. This pleasant state of affairs came to an end in 1898 when a rival club was formed under the presidency of Lady Marcus Beresford. Called The Cat Club, it had its own rules and ran its own shows, so splitting breeders and exhibitors into two factions and resulting in a great deal of confusion and anger.

After several troubled years, a special meeting of 19 delegates from the various clubs met in Westminster on 8 March 1910 and decided to form a new body called the Governing Council of the Cat Fancy (GCCF). The National Cat Club handed over all its powers to the new Council, enabling one register and one set of rules to be followed by the whole Cat Fancy. This body is run by an executive committee, and clubs and societies with sufficient members may become affiliated to the GCCF and send delegates to council meetings. It is still the main body for registering cats and holding shows in Britain.

British cat shows

Many cat shows take place each year all over the country and you can find details in the cat press. They last for one day, with exhibitors usually arriving between 8a.m. and 10a.m. The largest cat show in the world, run under GCCF rules, is held in London each year. It is organized by the National Cat Club, the club that started it all in the 19th century. Over 2,000 cats take part and each is judged in one open or breed class, as well as a range of miscellaneous classes and some classes offered by specialist breed clubs. Despite the size of the show, there is no climax to the proceedings, such as a Best in Show. Judging takes place in the body of the show hall, with each cat sitting anonymously in a numbered pen, allowed only a white blanket, white litter tray and water bowl. This procedure is common to all GCCF shows held in Britain.

GCCF judges are often breeders of long standing who have gained experience by stewarding for existing judges and are then nominated and approved by delegates at a Council meeting. They begin as probationer judges, assessing kittens, then progress to full judge status. Several GCCF judges are highly respected by other bodies and accept regular engagements to act as judges at cat shows held overseas.

Types of show

Championship show. Special Championship Challenge Certificates may be awarded to adult cats winning their open or breed classes. Neutered cats winning open classes may receive similar Premier Challenge Certificates. A cat winning three such certificates at three separate shows, awarded by three different judges, achieves Champion status. Champion cats and Premier neuters are entitled to affix their titles to their names. Full Champion cats can compete against one another in a special class to win Grand Challenge Certificates. Three such certificates, awarded by three different judges, make a cat a Grand Champion. Full Premier neuters have similar classes and can attain the rank of Grand Premier.

Sanction shows. These follow similar rules, but no Challenge Certificates are awarded and they are considered as dress rehearsals for the larger championship events.

Exemption shows. These enable newly-established clubs to gain experience in show management. They are more relaxed than the more important shows, with rules and classes of their own. For beginners, they are a good introduction to showing.

Classes

Open classes (open to all pedigree registered cats) are often divided into colours within breeds and are the most important classes of all. The winners of such classes are eligible for the Best of Breed awards at some shows, and a few offer a still higher award of Best in Show. Miscellaneous classes vary a good deal from show to show and you may enter any for which your cat is eligible. Classes may include:

Kitten	Young cat from 3–9 months
Adolescent	Cat between 9 and 15 months
Junior	Cat between 9 months and 2 years
Senior	Cat over 2 years
Veteran	Cat over 7 years
Novice	Exhibit not having won a first prize
Special limit	Exhibit not having won more than two first prizes
Limit	Exhibit not having won more than four first prizes

Debutante	Exhibit making its showing debut
Breeders	Exhibit bred by owner
Novice exhibitor	Must be exhibitor's first show

European cat shows

In Europe, most countries have at least two registering bodies, with one of them usually affiliated to the Federation Internationale Feline (FIFe). This is an enormous, incorporated and chartered body with affiliates in many parts of the world. It is managed by an executive board of experts, each elected to serve for a term of three years. The FIFe has three commissions – the judges' commission is responsible for the study of new breeds and their standards, the modification of existing standards for recognized breeds and the regulation of the stud-book; the show commission is responsible for efficient show management and the application of show rules and regulations; and the disciplinary commission hears complaints and problems from member countries and arbitrates in disputes. Fully established in 1949, today the FIFe is the largest cat body in the world, uniting more than 150,000 breeders and exhibitors in one cause – the love of the cat.

In most European countries, ring judging is common, but the rings are isolated from the show hall and the judges work in private. The cats are brought to them by highly trained stewards who carry the animals displayed along one forearm and gently restrain them with the opposite hand.

Entering your cat

Showing your cat means that you can have its type and potential assessed by experts and you can discover how your pet compares with others of the same breed. If you plan to breed cats, a show provides an opportunity for you to view possible stud males and talk to established breeders. A wise owner's introduction to a cat show is as a spectator; this way you can get the feel of the show, talk to experienced owners and perhaps take the opportunity to join a cat club. It is not always necessary to belong to a club or association in order to enter your cat for showing but you may find that you are only eligible for top awards or certain prizes if you are a member in good standing. Membership can bring other 'perks': you will be informed of shows for your breed or part of the country, you may get reduced entry fees, free vouchers for catalogues and access to an invaluable source of information. There is also a social side to club membership and you may discover that you become interested in the administrative and organizational side of showing and find yourself with an absorbing new hobby.

When you feel ready to start showing your cat, write to the show director or manager, enclosing a large stamped addressed envelope, asking for a schedule of the show that interests you, and an entry form. Make sure that you do this well in advance: entries for small shows usually close about three weeks before the event, and those for the larger shows, such as those run in Britain under the rules of the GCCF, may close a full two months before the show date.

Read the entry form and rules carefully, as classes and regulations vary. If you are unsure of the precise meaning of any of the terms used, consult an experienced breeder or the show manager. Show organizers sometimes publish specific times for handling telephone enquiries and you should always observe these and try to keep your enquiries as brief as possible, as organizers are usually busy people working in their spare time.

To enter pedigree classes, your pet must be registered with the appropriate authority. The breeder will normally have taken care of this but check if you are in any doubt and at the same time, make sure that you have registered the change of ownership. Copy the information required for the entry form carefully from the registration documents. The judging books and catalogues are compiled from this form, so it must be accurate and any mistakes may result in disqualification. Send the completed form to the show office with the appropriate fees and a stamped addressed envelope if you require an acknowledgement of your entry.

Preparing for the show

Judges are looking for health and excellent condition as well as conformity to the breed standard so preparing a cat for a show is an on-going process, aimed at producing a cat in peak condition on show day:

● Make sure that all vaccinations are up to date and that you have a certificate to prove it, as you may need to produce it.

● Ask your veterinary surgeon to check over the cat's teeth, ears and claws.

● Feed a good, well-balanced diet but do not make drastic changes in the weeks before the show, hoping to produce a fitter cat – this may result in gastric upsets instead.

● Groom your cat every day as the show approaches, in the manner recommended for the breed. Light-coloured cats are sometimes bathed, though it may be sufficient to wash and dry around the tail area to remove any staining. Dark-coloured cats may be given a bran bath but you must make sure that no trace of bran remains in the coat, or the cat will be disqualified. (For more details on grooming and bathing, see pages 43–5.) There are strict rules prohibiting plucking, shaving or colouring of the coat.

● Showing means that the cat will be handled by strangers and will be expected to remain calm and friendly, so if your cat normally meets few people, ask your friends and neighbours to come and handle it regularly. Those without pets of their own are best, as they are less likely to spread infection.

● If your cat is not used to travelling, start with a few short rehearsal trips, then make longer journeys until you are sure that the journey to the show will not leave your pet nervy and upset.

● Make sure that your cat is used to being confined in a small pen: rig up a rehearsal cage about the size of the show pen and keep your cat in it for a few minutes at first, then lengthen the time so that confinement on show day does not come as a shock.

● If the rules call for the cat to wear a numbered label or disc, you should see that it is used to wearing something round its neck, otherwise it may spend the whole show trying to get rid of it and working itself into a nervous state.

Show equipment

Assemble the equipment you will need before the day of the show:

Plain white blanket, without any trimmings, either wool or man-made fibre
Plain white litter tray
Litter, torn paper towels or toilet paper for tray
Plain white feeding and water bowls
Narrow white ribbon or tape to keep the identifying disc or label in place
Cat food or, if you do not want to give your cat a regular meal at the show, its favourite snacks
Water: it is wise to take water from home as your cat may refuse water that smells slightly different from normal
Brush and comb for grooming
Mild, non-toxic disinfectant and cloth
Vetting-in and passing out cards
Current vaccination certificate

If you have already been to a show you may have had an opportunity to buy the regulation style of equipment; otherwise you will probably find it advertised in the schedule, with details of mail-order services. In an on-floor judged show, you will not be allowed to add anything that would distinguish one pen from another.

The day of the show

Your cat should be taken to the show in a secure carrier, preferably the type that opens at the top so that the cat can be taken out and replaced with the minimum of fuss and without disarranging its coat. Arrive as early as possible for the vetting-in process: the longer the line of owners waiting with their cats, the greater the risk of infection. The veterinary surgeon will examine the cat for any parasites, any signs of deformity, disease or pregnancy in the female. The vet's decision is final and if your cat does not pass, it will not be allowed into the show hall. It can be a keen disappointment if your cat is turned away but it is essential that no risks are taken when so many cats are to spend the day in close proximity. If your cat passes the examination, the vetting-in slip will be signed and you can take your cat into the hall.

Inside the hall, you will find a pen with a number corresponding with your tally number; if the numbers are not consecutive, you will be able to consult a floor plan. Some owners like to disinfect the pen themselves, though this will have been done already by the organisers. Arrange your cat's equipment inside, with just a little litter or paper in the tray at first. After a long journey your cat will probably want to use the tray and you can then refill it with fresh litter for the rest of the day. You will then want to complete last minute grooming before owners have to leave the hall for the judging to begin.

At shows run under GCCF rules, judges and their stewards go to each pen in turn, take out the cat and place it on a small portable table for assessment. To help to check the cat's profile and eye colour, as well as its weight and muscular development, the judge will probably hold it at eye level. The judge will write a critique of each cat, with reference to an official standard of points for its breed. After handling each exhibit, hands and table are disinfected before passing on to the next cat. Once each cat in the class has been assessed, judges place them in order of merit, awarding first, second and third prizes, followed by a reserve. The results are taken to the show administration table, where they are entered into the awards book; the show secretary keeps one copy while another is posted on the awards board for the information of the exhibitors. Winners may receive rosettes or small money prizes and if there are Best of Breed and Best in Show awards, the victorious cats may receive a silver trophy or some other special prize. There may also be Very Highly Commended, Highly Commended and Commended awards but they do not carry prize money or rosettes. Though you are not allowed to speak to the judges or stewards while judging is in progress, they will usually be willing to discuss your cat's good and bad features later.

Once you get your pet home after the show, you should make sure that it has plenty of time to rest and relax for two or three days. Watch carefully for any signs of infection and if you see any symptoms, consult your veterinary surgeon immediately. The veterinary inspection at the show, and the precautions taken, mean that your cat is unlikely to pick up any infection but if this does happen, you should inform the show organisers.

Most cats enjoy an outing to a cat show, or at least tolerate it without any ill-effects but some never seem to get used to the noise and the staring eyes. If you do find that your cat hates the whole business, do not force it to go to show after show. Buy a kitten that can be trained for showing, or offer your services as an administrator or steward to enjoy your involvement in the wider world of the cat show.